THE WORLD
OF
WATCHES

This edition published by
CHARTWELL BOOK
A division of BOOK SALES, Inc
114 Northfield Avenue
Edison, New Jersey 08837
First English language edition, 1996
© Copyright, Paris, 1995

ISBN : 0-7858-0743-8

Printed in Spain

THE WORLD OF WATCHES

Gilles Lhote
Jean Lassaussois

CONTENTS

FOREWORD

The world of watches is both a fascinating and complex one. This book is an invitation to the reader to explore this wonderful world and share in our passion for great timepieces and their distinguished creators. We have chosen to focus on the world's most legendary models, both classic and avant-garde, and the prestigious watchmakers, past and present, who have produced – and who continue to produce – true and lasting works of art. The watches featured in these pages were selected for their quality, originality, unique characteristics and charm.

Our journey through time begins with an introduction to the mechanical watches of yesteryear, those living legends so coveted by today's avid collectors. Our travels inevitably take us to the valleys of Switzerland, cradle of the watchmaking industry, where great craftsmen have devoted nearly two centuries to the pursuit of absolute perfection.

The watchmakers and watches highlighted in this book include: Audemars Piguet and their Royal Oak Number 001 model, a unique piece which all watch devotees dream of possessing one day; Baume & Mercier and their Fleetwood model; Abraham Louis-Breguet, the ingenious French inventor who became one of the world's most renowned watchmakers; Leon Breitling and his passion for aeronautics, featuring the highly acclaimed Old Navitimer; Louis Cartier who, in 1904, invented an elegant and functional watch for his friend the aviator Santos-Dumont which would transcend generations; Hamilton in America, who originated pocket watches for the railway pioneers, and later became official supplier to the US army (their stainless steel watches were worn by the GIs who disembarked on the shores of Normandy); IWC and the development of the Jones movement which culminated in the exquisite Destriero Scafusia, the 21-function watch-chronograph; the internationally established Jaeger-LeCoultre, most often associated with the Reverso, but also manufacturers of movements for the most prestigious watches in the world; Longines, another avid aviation enthusiast, who will forever be associated with Charles Lindbergh and the horary angle watch; Omega who forged a historic and worldwide reputation when Neil Armstrong walked on the moon with its Speedmaster; Patek Philippe who designed the most complicated masterpieces in the profession; Rolex who scored a coup when Mercedes Gleitze swam the English Channel wearing the first waterproof watch, the Rolex Oyster (the Rolex Prince and dual-dial Prince Railways followed soon after). To this exceptional list we have chosen to add Swatch, not only because the company has sold 100 million models in just ten years, but also because it is the revolutionary watch of modern times – a daring, provocative, high-quality timepiece and the prize of many collectors, who have snapped them up with well-publicized enthusiasm. Then there is TAG Heuer with its famous "avant-garde techniques" which led it to triumph on Olympic fields and race tracks. Our expedition culminates with Zenith, father of the incomparable El Primero, a chronograph fitted with an automatic movement of 38,000 vibrations per hour.

Many collectors and watch lovers may be surprised that we have not included pocket watches on our list. Given the sheer number and diversity of these first witnesses of time, that endeavour begs an entirely separate work.

MECHANICAL MASTERPIECES

There was once a time when many a master watchmaker would have sold his soul for the secret of producing a self-winding watch. In today's technological age, it sometimes seems as if there's nothing left to discover or invent. The paradoxical reaction to this is an increasing nostalgia for good, old-fashioned mechanical watches. Whether this yearning is merely a passing whim of fashion or a real resurgence of the past remains to be seen. The watches featured here still tick away with supreme accuracy, driven by superb mechanics which have stood the test of time. Whether their mechanisms are simple or complicated, these beautiful timepieces are fascinating to watch lovers of the quartz age. They possess that certain charm exuded by objects that have witnessed the passage of time. Their power of seduction lies in the detail, the design, the elegance of the case, the finesse of the dial, the shape of the strap or, quite simply, in the way they feel or even smell. Collectors canvas the globe, as if in search of a rare bird, to acquire one of these coveted timepieces. Each has his or her fetish: some are obsessed with military watches; some dream only of aviation chronographs or "grandes complications" (the term used by professionals in reference to particularly complicated movements created by reputed watchmakers); some seek out the artistic beauty of ladies' dress watches; while others concentrate their efforts on pocket watches and chronometers. But all collectors have one thing in common: a passion for the mechanical timepiece. You don't need to be an expert or incredibly wealthy to be a watch collector. All it takes is plenty of enthusiasm, tenacity and something of the hunter's instinct. This first chapter features a selection of well-loved and sought-after antique watches while in the following chapters the great names in watchmaking are represented by a selection of their legendary creations.

This stainless steel wristwatch is an Auricoste type 20 military chronograph, a model used by the French army between 1950 and 1955. It features two small dials, one for minutes located at three o'clock and one for seconds at nine o'clock, as well as an instantaneous reset button for the flying second hand, a Plexiglas crystal and a screwed back.

This classic 1970s mechanical Omega features a round crystal watchglass, white dial, and Roman numerals. It is shown here on a black crocodile strap.

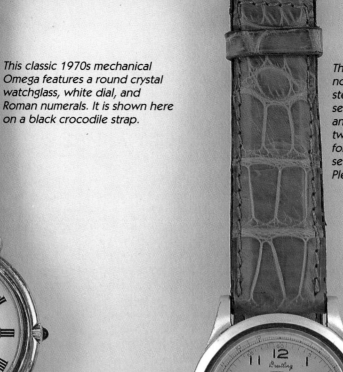

This 1950s Breitling chronograph has a steel case and features several tachometric and telemetric scales, two small dials – one for minutes and one for seconds – and a Plexiglas crystal.

This elegant barrel-shaped model by Longines, is a mechanical Curvex watch which dates back to the 1940s. It has a gold case, crystal watch-glass and crocodile strap. The hand-painted Arabic numerals are an original feature.

Another Longines watch, from the Conquest series manufactured between 1960 and 1965, with gold case, automatic movement, date display located at twelve o'clock, second hand and leather strap

This extremely rare mechanical Longines watch with gold case and enamelled dial was manufactured in 1920. The second hand is located at six o'clock and it is attached to a gold ostrich leather strap. The distinctive features

of this 1950s Longines chronograph with steel case are its single push-piece situated at two o'clock and the absence of a minute dial. It is equipped with several tachometric and telemetric scales. The strap is ostrich leather.

This Elgin watch with chased silver case, second hand at six o'clock and Arabic numerals, dates back to the 1920s. Elgin was first established in 1864, and continued to produce watches until the 1950s.

1930s Pierce chrono-graph, featuring st_less steel case wit_ single pusher at fo_ o'clock and minut_ dial at twelve o'cl__ There is a central second hand, as v_ as a small second located at six o'clo_ This 1950s Lindbe_

model by Longines has a central dial, designed so that the plane's position can be calculated by the horary angle. It can be adjusted with the pusher located at two o'clock.

1940s Longines ladies' watch with gold-plated case and mechanical movement. This particular model has a distinctive interior bezel, which can be regulated with the pusher located at two o'clock.

LONGINES AND OTHER MODELS

A rare Longines split-second 1940s chronograph. The supplementary or fly-back second hand performs a double time-keeping function or it can be used to calculate an intermediate time. It also indicates hourly intervals divided into 100ths.

A 1950s gold-cased Movado. Its originality lies in the day/month/date display. The days of the month are situated around the perimeter of the dial and indicated by a hand. The day and the month appear in the two displays. This watch is attached to a gold ostrich leather strap.

1950s Auricoste military chronograph, made for the French army. The steel case has a screwed back and the second hand instantly resets. There are two small dials at six and nine o'clock and the crystal is Plexiglas.

The celebrated Breitling Old Navitimer chronograph in steel dates back to the 1960s. It is equipped with a bidirectional bezel and a type-52 slide rule. Three small dials are situated at three, six and nine o'clock.

ANTIQUE WATCHES

AVIATION CHRONOGRAPHS

The 1950s German Junghans chronograph is made of steel and fitted with a bi-directional, graduated bezel. The minute dial is situated at three o'clock and the second dial is at nine o'clock.

This steel Hanhart model was manufactured in Germany in the late 1930s. Soldiers and navigators (but not pilots) used this timepiece during the Second World War. It has a special feature - when the watch is reset, the second hand stops to strike the hour.

A rare steel Breguet aviation chronograph with three dials. The minute dial, situated at three o'clock, divides the time into twenty-minute intervals. It is larger than the other two to facilitate reading.

This Hanhart military chronograph was used during the Second World War by pilots in the German airforce. The movement is mechanical and the case is made of steel and brass and has a knurled crown.

The type-21 Dodane military chronograph, used by the French army in the 1950s, has a bidirectional black bezel which is anti-reflective. The 30-minute dial is situated at three o'clock, while the second dial is at nine o'clock.

This beautiful mechanical Vulcain steel chronograph dates from the 1930s. It is of particular interest because of the single push-piece situated at two o'clock and its original steel attachments.

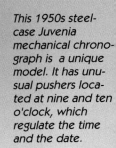

This 1950s steel-case Juvenia mechanical chronograph is a unique model. It has unusual pushers located at nine and ten o'clock, which regulate the time and the date.

ANTIQUE WATCHES

MECHANICAL CHRONOGRAPHS

The 1965 Baume & Mercier classic chronograph, with mechanical movement. The case is gold-plated and the dial is silver. The 30-minute dial is at three o'clock while the second dial is located at nine o'clock. The strap is crocodile leather.

This magnificent 1930s gold Omega chronograph has a mechanical movement and white enamel dial. The single pusher which controls the s and reset functions is locate two o'clock.

This 1950s steel mechanical Omega chronograph features a 30-minute dial situated at three o'clock and a second dial at nine o'clock. Attached here to a crocodile strap with matt finish.

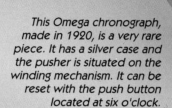

This Omega chronograph, made in 1920, is a very rare piece. It has a silver case and the pusher is situated on the winding mechanism. It can be reset with the push button located at six o'clock.

This beautiful gold Angelus mechanical chronograph was manufactured in the 1950s. The 45-minute dial is situated at three o'clock and the second dial is at nine o'clock. It is attached to a golden brown ostrich leather strap.

When it first appeared in the 1950s, this Breitling was known as the Premier model. It features a screwed back and three dials located at three, six and nine o'clock. The hands are luminescent and it is attached to a leather strap.

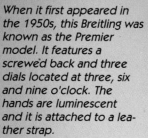

Longines military watch, manufactured in 1945, with mechanical movement and steel case. The small second dial, located at six o'clock, stops when the watch is reset. The hands and numbers are luminescent.

This mechanical watch was made in 1925 by American watchmaker Waltham. It has a steel case, the hands are luminescent and there is a small second dial at six o'clock.

MICKEY MOUSE AND COCA-COLA

Gold Breitling watch made in 1950 with screwed back, attached to a crocodile leather strap. The luminescent hands and numbers are protected by a Plexiglas crystal.

This very rare American Coca-Cola promotional watch dates back to 1940 and was manufactured by either Hamilton or Elgin. It has a mechanical movement, gold-plated case and luminescent hands.

The make of this exceedingly rare timepiece, which dates right back to the beginning of the century, is unknown. It has a silver case and enamel dial and the crystal watchgalss is protected by a honeycombed cover.

This very rare American Mickey Mouse watch was made in 1925. It has a steel case and the hours and minutes are pointed to by the helpful hands of Disney's legendary mouse.

This Movado ladies' chronometer was manufactured in 1950. It has screw attachments and a gold and steel case. The movement is mechanical with the second hand situated at six o'clock.

Mido mechanical watch, 1945. This top-quality model features a small second hand at six o'clock as well as luminescent hands and numbers. This Jaeger steel chronogra-

...ph with mechanical movement, marketed in the 1960s, features dials at three, six and nine o'clock and a central second hand.

This magnificent gold-plated mechanical 1950s Pierce chronograph features a column wheel chronograph movement. It is equipped with a minute dial at twelve o'clock, a central second hand and a small second dial situated at six o'clock.

1950s Doxa mechanical chronograph in gold and steel. It boasts three telemetric and tachometric scales and the pulsometer is located on the dial. The hands and numbers are luminescent.

The strap attachments on this 1950s gold mechanical chronograph are what make it such a unique model. It features a tachometric scale and two dials: the 30-minute dial is located at three o'clock and the second dial at nine o'clock.

This outstanding Universal Genève steel Aérocompax model is equipped with twelve-hour and 30-minute dials, and a second dial located at nine o'clock. The most extraordinary feature of this 1950s model is the twelve o'clock dial, a second watchface which may be set to remind its wearer of a scheduled appointment.

The 1960s Baume & Mercier gold-plated mechanical chronograph, with three tachometric scales, two round pushers and two dials located at three and nine o'clock which indicate minutes and seconds respectively.

CHRONOGRAPHS OF THE 50S AND 60S

This 1950s mechanical chronometer has a single pusher located between one and two o'clock. The same button activates stop and reset functions. The chronograph cannot be restarted once it has been stopped. It must always be set back to zero.

Mechanical steel 1950s chronograph by Longines, with copper dial and pushed back, leather strap and Plexiglas crystal.

This 1950s Juvenia mechanical chronograph in steel features three dials. The hour dial is at six o'clock, the minute dial at three o'clock and the second dial at nine o'clock. It is attached to an ostrich leather strap.

1950s Longines mechanical watch with steel case, silver dial, Arabic numerals and indexes. It has a small second dial at six o'clock, a Plexiglas crystal and a crocodile strap.

This small mechanical chronograph was made by Eterna in the 1950s and features a black dial with two small inner dials for the minutes and the seconds. The Arabic numerals are luminescent and the strap is leather.

This little mechanical military watch was manufactured by Longines in the 1940s. The second hand is located at six o'clock and stops when the watch is reset. It has a black dial and luminescent Arabic numerals.

This handsome Juvenia mechanical chronograph 4 with three small dials was manufactured in the 1950s. It features a triple day/month/date calendar. The day and month appear in the two displays while a red hand indicates the date along the perimeter of the dial. The buttons located at nine and ten o'clock regulate these functions.

This Longines mechanical chronograph boasts an unusual copper dial. The second hand is situated at nine o'clock and the 30-minute dial is at three o'clock. It has a Plexiglas crystal and leather strap.

CHRONOGRAPHS OF DISTINCTION

This 1940s Vulcain mechanical chronometer in steel is equipped with a rectangular single push-piece located at two o'clock. The second dial is located at nine o'clock and the minute dial at three o'clock. Roman numerals, screw attachments and a crocodile strap add to the classic appeal of this model.

This superb gold Jaeger mechanical chronograph was made in 1940. On the copper dial, the 30-minute, hour and second dials are located at three, six and nine o'clock respectively.

This model in yellow gold from the Cintrée Curvex collection is typical of the Franck Muller style. It is a mechanical chronograph with a manual winding mechanism. The case and watchglass are curved at the six–twelve hour and three–nine hour axes.

This mechanical chronograph in platinum was entirely handmade by Franck Muller, and was the second model created by the master watchmaker. It features a perpetual calendar with lunar phases and equation of time. It is programmed until the year 2100.

EXCEPTIONAL WATCHES

CITY WATCHES

This Breitling gold chronograph with perpetual calendar comes from the Old Navitimer collection. It is a complex model fitted with a bidirectional rotating bezel with a type-52 aviation slide rule. Programmed to the year 2100, it indicates lunar phases, seasons, weeks, year, date, day and month.

Designed by IWC, this exquisite ultra-slim mechanical model in platinum features a perpetual calendar with lunar phases. The day/date/month/year are regulated by a single pusher.

This gold American Tank watch by Cartier is programmed accurately to track the exact length of each month. The date is indicated by the small dial situated at twelve o'clock. This model is attached to a crocodile strap.

A perpetual gold calendar watch by Piaget. This ultra-slim automatic model indicates the day, month, date and lunar phase. It is attached to a crocodile strap.

This Piaget automatic chronograph in gold features a split-second function. The extra second hand, known as the fly-back hand, can be used for double time-keeping or the calculation of an intermediary period of time. The two second hands may be stopped independently of one another and are controlled by the pusher located at ten o'clock.

AUDEMARS PIGUET
MASTERS OF THE COMPLICATION

On 17 December 1881, Jules Louis Audemars and Edward Auguste Piguet sealed a contract with their respective coats of arms and endorsed the partnership the following year with the manufacture of the Audemars Piguet official stamp. That same year, the master watchmakers from Brassus, Switzerland, designed their first "Grande Complication". In 1885, they put their highly complicated pocket watches on the market and by 1928, just one year before the Great Depression brought the world to its knees, Audemars Piguet had established a solid reputation and international renown, reflected in the publicity poster they produced around this time. It featured three very sober-looking and complex watches under which ran the words: "Represented in Paris, London, New York, Berlin, Buenos Aires." This enviable reputation was in fact built on the creation of a watch presented at the Universal Exhibition in Paris in 1889. It was a masterpiece featuring a minute repeater, perpetual calendar and split-second chronograph. Just as Audemars Piguet had weathered the watchmaking crisis in 1909 and the First World War, it would also survive the collapse of Wall Street and the Second World War. The manufacturer approached the post-war market with prestigious, highly complicated watches, and nursed itself back to financial health. The great masterpiece of this period was the "Grande Complication", sought after by wealthy clients the world over, undeterred by the fact that they had to wait months, even years, to own one of these pieces.

In 1972, Audemars Piguet introduced the Royal Oak steel watch with a 21-carat gold rotor, which is still a market leader today. While the use of quartz dramatically reduced prices and caused an unprecedented crisis, Audemars Piguet responded with luxury models and greater complications, introducing Dual Time in 1981, tourbillon watches in 1986 and the incomparable Star Wheel in 1992. One of the company's most recent models, the automatic Triple Complication, proves once and for all that the grand tradition of watchmaking has withstood the test of time.

The 51-jewel Royal Oak automatic chronograph, Offshore model, 1993. It has a steel case and strap, tachometric scale, a frequency of 28,600 vibrations per hour, 40-hour reserve and is waterproof to 325 feet.

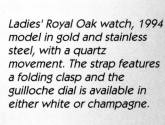

Ladies' Royal Oak watch, 1994 model in gold and stainless steel, with a quartz movement. The strap features a folding clasp and the guilloche dial is available in either white or champagne.

Men's automatic Royal Oak, 1992 model. Steel case on a leather strap with guilloche dial, luminescent indexes and hands, and screwed crown. Waterproof to 160 feet.

THE ROYAL OAK SERIES

Ladies' Royal Oak quartz watch with 18-carat gold case. This model came out in 1994.

Men's Royal Oak in tantalum and rose gold. This model dates from 1993.

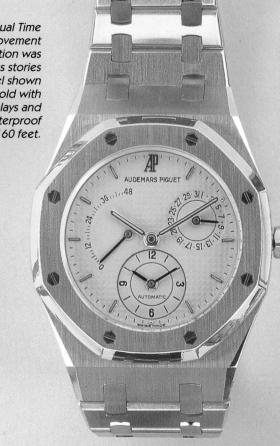

The Royal Oak Dual Time with automatic movement and reserve indication was one of the success stories of 1992. The model shown here is 18-carat gold with two time zone displays and a date dial. It is waterproof to 160 feet.

This Royal Oak steel quartz watch appeared in 1985. The hours are marked with diamond indexes and the strap features a safety clasp. It is waterproof to 325 feet.

Royal Oak Dual Time in steel and gold, 1991. The technical specifications are the same as for the solid gold model.

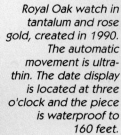

Royal Oak watch in tantalum and rose gold, created in 1990. The automatic movement is ultra-thin. The date display is located at three o'clock and the piece is waterproof to 160 feet.

This Royal Oak Dual Time, unveiled in 1991, is made from steel and features an automatic movement. It is waterproof to 160 feet.

Created in 1983, this superb stainless steel Royal Oak indicates the day, month, date and lunar phase, and tracks leap years. It is waterproof to 65 feet.

THE ROYAL OAK SERIES

The 1984 steel Royal Oak automatic features a simple day/date calendar indicating lunar phase. It is waterproof to 325 feet.

This ultra-thin ladies' Royal Oak was produced in 1985. It features an automatic movement and the strap is completely handmade.

Men's Royal Oak gold and diamond quartz watch, 1987 model. The diamonds encrusted on the dial and bezel are round while baguette diamonds decorate the strap links. Waterproof to 160 feet.

This ladies' Royal Oak quartz model is identical to the men's model opposite, except for the baguette diamonds which do not feature on this strap.

28

Ladies' Royal Oak quartz model, in gold and stainless steel with diamond-encrusted bezel. There are ten diamond indexes on the dial.

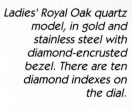

Ultra-slim ladies' Royal Oak quartz model, with bezel in white gold inlaid with diamonds. The mother-of-pearl dial features diamond indexes, three of which are baguette diamonds.

*Ladies' Royal Oak
quartz watch, 1980
model, with handmade
18-carat gold case
and strap.*

*Men's Royal Oak with
quartz movement, 1985
model, with handmade
18-carat gold case
and strap.*

DELUXE
MODELS

*Ladies' Royal Oak, 1985
model, with automatic
winding mechanism. The
case and strap are
18-carat gold.*

*Men's Royal Oak, 1990
model, with an
automatic winding
mechanism. The case
and strap are
18-carat gold.*

Very rare perpetual calendar skeleton watch with mechanical movement in chased yellow gold and visible wheelworks. This piece was created in 1993 and is one of the company's most complicated models.

AUDEMARS PIGUET
COMPLICATED MODELS

Launched in 1991, this movement with perpetual calendar is both the slimmest and smallest in the world. The rectangular case is reminiscent of 1920s design.

Automatic chronograph, 1994 model, featuring a perpetual calendar with lunar phase and platinum bezel inlaid with diamonds.

This is the extremely rare yellow gold Star Wheel which appeared in 1991. It has an automatic movement and the hours are indicated by pivoting discs in engraved crystal, while the minutes appear at the top of the dial. The time on this watch, for example, is 11:45.

The classic calendar watch with mechanical winding mechanism, created in 1983, features a yellow gold case, two day/date dials and a lunar phase display situated at six o'clock. This model is waterproof to 95 feet.

Created in 1978, this gold watch features a perpetual day/date/month calendar which also indicates the lunar phase.

This automatic Dual Time watch in yellow gold, first introduced in 1990, features a double time zone function and a power reserve indicator. The date appears on the small dial located at two o'clock.

This rare gold skeleton watch features a perpetual calendar that indicates the day/month/date and lunar phase. The crocodile strap has a gold folding clasp.

This magnificent chronograph in 18-carat gold was created in 1985, and its automatic movement is equipped with a 21-carat gold rotor. The date display is located at three o'clock and the perimeter of the dial features a tachometric scale. The black crocodile strap has a folding clasp.

BAUME & MERCIER
QUALITY AND STYLE

Baume was the name on everybody's lips at the various international exhibitions held between 1834 and 1914 and their chronographs swept up an enviable number of awards. At the end of the First World War, William Baume, director of the Horologerie des Blois in Switzerland joined forces with Paul Mercier, and together Baume and Mercier continued their quest for aesthetically pleasing, high quality timepieces. In the Forties, the company was taken over by Constantin de Gorsky, an acute businessman who concentrated on the development of a ladies' dress watch collection. The company continued to enjoy commercial success in France as well as in England and throughout the British Empire, largely thanks to their elegant and distinctive chronographs which featured complete calendars as well as tachometric and telemetric scales. Certain models, designed to suit the tastes and needs of travellers and businessmen, even featured a special dial designed uniquely for monitoring telephone signals. Then, in the early Sixties, Piaget breathed new life into Baume & Mercier, and the company began to enjoy something of a renaissance. They concentrated on the manufacture of ultra-slim watches and elegant ladies' designs. The following decade saw the creation of the legendary Riviera with its twelve-sided case, which was to become the company's leading design. Other successful collections followed: Linéa, Absolu and Shogun. The Nineties began in a wave of luxury with the Transpacific and Fleetwood models, alongside new collections of ladies' chronographs in gold and steel. Quality and style have always been, and continue to be, the basis of the Baume and Mercier philosophy.

The 1994 Hampton steel watch has an elegant rectangular case and a strap with folding clasp. It features a Swiss quartz movement, sapphire crystal and copper dial with a second hand at six o'clock. This watch also comes with white and anthracite dials, and can be attached to a leather strap with or without a folding clasp.

The 1973 Riviera model has a twelve-sided silver case, one side for each hour. It exists in a quartz version and is also available with automatic movement.

The Transpacific chronograph in gold and steel with automatic movement first appeared in 1990. Its scratchproof sapphire crystal features a loupe over the date display at three o'clock for easy reading. It is also available with a white dial.

HAMPTON, RIVIERA, TRANSPACIFIC

The quartz Riviera watch, made in 1973, has a steel strap and dodecagonal case. The sapphire crystal protects a white face which features Roman numerals. It is waterproof up to 95 feet.

The Destra automatic watch-chronograph, created in 1993, is one of the models from the 1991 Baume & Mercier sports line. There is a tachometric scale engraved on the outer bezel. The date display is at three o'clock and the three dials are situated at six, nine and twelve o'clock.

This ladies' watch from the Linéa collection was created by Baume & Mercier in 1987. It has a gold-plated and steel case and is one of the company's most successful models.

This ladies' model is also from the Linéa collection. It has a quartz movement and the sapphire crystal protects a black dial. The steel strap fastens with a folding clasp.

Men's model from the Linéa collection, shown with a steel case and strap. Quartz movement, waterproof to 95 feet.

This Linéa line men's watch has a steel case and strap. The dial is white and it features the same technical specifications as the other Linea models.

This superb Bagatelle model, with 18-carat gold case and strap, runs on a quartz movement. It features a sapphire crystal, white face and Roman numerals.

This model is from the Monthillaut collection. It has a gold case and bright Louisiana crocodile strap, and runs on a quartz movement. It is waterproof to 95 feet.

Original ladies' model from the Linéa line, with gold-plated case and strap, and mother-of-pearl dial. In September 1995, this model was replaced by an updated version in solid gold.

This quartz model features a gold bezel and an iridescent grey guilloche dial. It is waterproof to 95 feet.

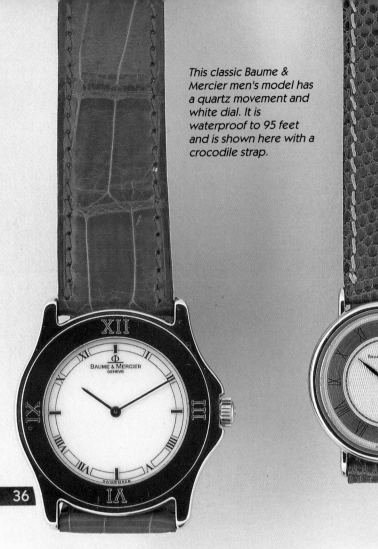

This classic Baume & Mercier men's model has a quartz movement and white dial. It is waterproof to 95 feet and is shown here with a crocodile strap.

Ladies' model from the Richemont collection, attached to a saddle-stitched matt lizard strap. It features a grey dial, Roman numerals and a sapphire crystal, and is waterproof to 95 feet.

The 1994 steel-cased Hampton model with quartz movement. This version has an anthracite dial with a second hand at six o'clock, and is attached to a leather strap with steel folding clasp.

This steel Transpacific has three blue dials, but the model is also available with a tachometric scale on the outer bezel, in place of the Roman numerals shown here.

The men's Riviera watch is easily identified by its dodecagonal (twelve-sided) case. It has an automatic movement and is attached to a crocodile strap with folding clasp.

Baume & Mercier
ladies' Riviera model,
created in 1973,
with steel case and
strap, and quartz
movement.

Ultra-slim quartz watch
with gold case and
champagne-coloured
ial. It features a sapphire
crystal and lizard strap.

Baume & Mercier gold-
plated and steel Linéa men's
watch. Since its introduction
onto the market in 1987,
this model has become one
of the company's landmark
designs.

Ladies' Linéa, with
steel dial and strap.
This model features
the same technical
specifications as
the Linéa models
shown on the
preceding pages.

The ladies' dress
Riviera, with
diamond-encrusted
bezel. This model is
waterproof to
95 feet.

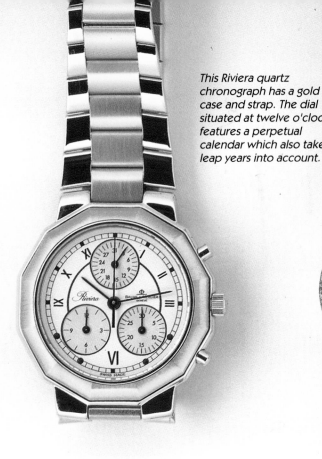

This Riviera quartz chronograph has a gold case and strap. The dial situated at twelve o'clock features a perpetual calendar which also takes leap years into account.

The Corinthe ladies' quartz model, with gold case inlaid with diamonds. Note the two sapphires embedded in the strap fittings at twelve and six o'clock. The mother-of-pearl dial also has four diamond indexes.

This is the jewelled version of the Birmane ladies' model. A triad of rubies, sapphires and emeralds sparkle at twelve and six o'clock; the bezel is inlaid with diamonds and the strap is solid gold.

The Absolu ladies' model, with quartz movement, rectangular 18-carat gold case and honeycomb strap. It has a sapphire crystal and a white dial with Roman numerals.

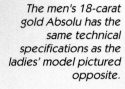

The men's 18-carat gold Absolu has the same technical specifications as the ladies' model pictured opposite.

The Riviera quartz chronograph, with gold case and strap, and programmed perpetual movement. It boasts the same technical specifications as the other models in the Riviera chronograph range.

This jewelled model has a diamond-encrusted bezel and twelve diamond indexes. It is mounted on a 'rice grain' strap. This quartz watch is waterproof to 95 feet.

THE JEWELLED COLLECTION

The bezel of this Bohême ladies' model boasts a double row of inlaid diamonds. The gold strap features two diamond triads on each attachment.

The Ephèse ladies' model features a diamond-encrusted bezel and sapphire baguettes on the attachments at twelve and six o'clock, as well as twelve diamond indexes. Waterproof to 95 feet.

Another model from the Bohême series, this piece features the same specifications as the watch opposite, the only variations being the sapphire attachments and white dial.

Model from the sports line launched between 1972 and 1973, with an exceptional Accutron Diapason movement (the predecessor to quartz) featuring a frequency of 300 Hertz. The two displays indicating the day and date are situated at three o'clock.

1930s square automatic watch with a central second hand. The gold case and squared crystal watchglass are convex.

1960s mechanical watch with a gold case, second hand at six o'clock, Plexiglas crystal and Roman numerals.

This splendid steel 1940s chronograph features date and lunar phase displays. The day and the month appear in the two displays located at twelve o'clock. A hand indicates the date, located on the outer rim of the dial.

This beautiful 1960s automatic model features a white gold square case attached to a leather strap.

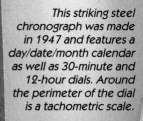

This striking steel chronograph was made in 1947 and features a day/date/month calendar as well as 30-minute and 12-hour dials. Around the perimeter of the dial is a tachometric scale.

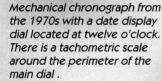

Small, square 1940s chronograph in gold with a mechanical movement. The 30-minute dial is located at three o'clock and the second dial is at nine o'clock, with a central second hand.

Mechanical chronograph from the 1970s with a date display dial located at twelve o'clock. There is a tachometric scale around the perimeter of the main dial .

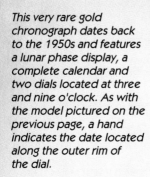

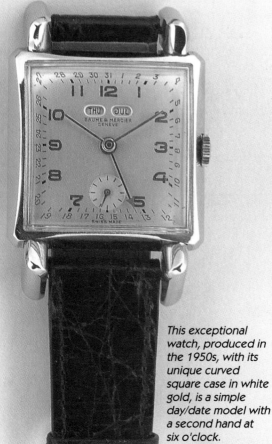

This very rare gold chronograph dates back to the 1950s and features a lunar phase display, a complete calendar and two dials located at three and nine o'clock. As with the model pictured on the previous page, a hand indicates the date located along the outer rim of the dial.

This exceptional watch, produced in the 1950s, with its unique curved square case in white gold, is a simple day/date model with a second hand at six o'clock.

INVENTOR OF GENIUS

The house of Breguet has accumulated an impressive roster of customers over the last two centuries: Marie Antoinette, Louis XVIII, Napoleon I, Frederick-William of Prussia, Princess Murat, Poniatowski, Marlborough, Rothschild, Alexander Dumas, Arthur Rubinstein, Bugatti, Winston Churchill and King Farouk to name but a few. The list of emperors, queens, kings, heads of state, princes, dukes, counts, generals, artists, writers and athletes who have sworn by Breguet is endless.

One Breguet masterpiece, engraved with the words "Régulateur à tourbillon" on the back of its gold case, was bought by Count Stanislav Potocki of Saint Petersburg in 1809 for the princely sum of 4,600 francs. The exquisite timepiece was equipped with the latest complications of the day: a second hand and a power reserve. It entered into Breguet legend, as the famous watch commissioned in 1783 by Marie Antoinette had done before it. This was a historic automatic timepiece complete with perpetual calendar, minute repeater, equation of time, thermometer and power reserve, sadly stolen from The Institute of Islamic Art in Jerusalem in 1983. The ingenious "watchmaker to the navy" left his indelible mark on the industry with the invention in 1790 of the shock resistant timepiece, which made watches more resilient to the wearer's motions, followed by the spiral and tourbillon (literally 'whirlwind') mechanism in 1795, and the detached constant-force escapement in 1798. He also invented the double-barrel marine chronometer. Following his death in 1823, the Breguet reins were taken up first by his son and then by his nephew, who later formed a partnership with the Brown family of England, entering into Breguet legend in his own right. In 1946, the finishing touches were put to the gold tourbillon chronometer, model number 3357, sold in 1959 to L.H. Dulles for 9,000 francs. New generations of tourbillon skeleton watches, Marine automatics and watches with equation of time soon followed. To this day, Breguet still enjoys a large and faithful following.

In 1815, Abraham-Louis Breguet was commissioned as the official supplier to the navy, an event commemorated by a special line of watches and chronographs. This 18-carat gold Marine automatic chronograph, which weighs 2.15 ounces, is attached to a blue crocodile strap with a folding clasp. The distinctive Breguet hands are the watchmaker's hallmark.

The 1992 medium Marine automatic watch, in gold with gold strap. The bezel and the central links of the strap are inlaid with diamonds, as are the horns of the case. The dial is mother-of-pearl and the date display is located at six o'clock.

This automatic chronograph from the Marine collection (5.2 ounces of 18-carat gold were used for the case) was first launched in 1991 in Basel, Switzerland.

This automatic ladies' Marine watch in gold and steel is from the 1993 Breguet collection.

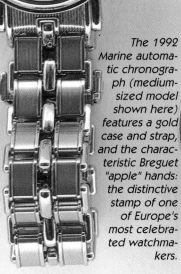

1988 Marine automatic with 18-carat gold case and strap and 21-carat gold interior rotor. The date display is at six o'clock and it is waterproof to 160 feet.

The 1992 Marine automatic chronograph (medium-sized model shown here) features a gold case and strap, and the characteristic Breguet "apple" hands: the distinctive stamp of one of Europe's most celebrated watchmakers.

The 1992 automatic watch in gold, with perpetual calendar and equation of time. The arrow located between one and two o'clock indicates the difference between mean solar time and real solar time. The day display is located at twelve o'clock. The calendar can be regulated with the corrector attached to the strap.

Automatic platinum watch with perpetual calendar, created in 1987. The calendar is regulated by a corrector attached to the strap. The lunar phase dial is located at six o'clock. Each model is numbered both on the dial and on the back of the case.

This automatic platinum watch with lunar phase and day/date/month displays was created in 1981. The serpentine hand on the dial indicates the date.

This platinum chronograph created in 1984 has a 30-minute and a second dial situated at three and nine o'clock respectively.

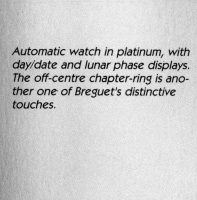

Automatic watch in platinum, with day/date and lunar phase displays. The off-centre chapter-ring is another one of Breguet's distinctive touches.

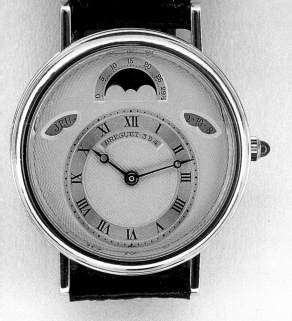

THE COMPLICATIONS

This platinum and rose gold watch launched in 1987 has a visible tourbillon movement. The chapter-ring is off-centre and this particular model also features the master watchmaker's secret signature.

White gold watch with visible tourbillon and chased solid silver back. Created in 1989, this watch features the same technical specifications as the tourbillon model pictured above.

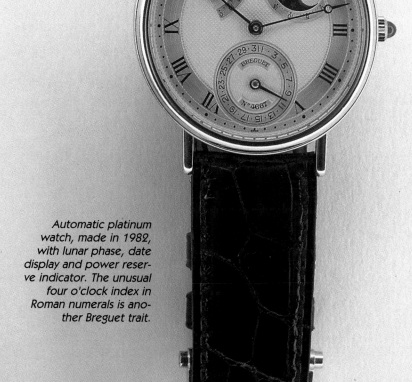

Automatic platinum watch, made in 1982, with lunar phase, date display and power reserve indicator. The unusual four o'clock index in Roman numerals is another Breguet trait.

A rare and exceptional skeleton watch with the Breguet tourbillon complication. The case is made of white gold and the chapter-ring is off-centre.

The reverse side of the skeleton tourbillon watch, with transparent back revealing the intricacy of its handmade and hand-engraved mechanics. The work of a veritable master.

Mechanical watch in yellow gold, created in 1986, with an off-centre lunar phase indicator and a small second hand located at six o'clock.

Automatic watch in yellow gold, made in 1986, with small central hour-circle and date display located at six o'clock.

Classic yellow gold watch, produced in 1982, has an automatic movement and is remarkably slim. This model is attached to a black crocodile strap.

THE CLASSIC COM-PLICATIONS

Mechanical watch in yellow gold, created in 1989, with power reserve and small second hand at six o'clock. Attached to a black crocodile strap.

Mechanical watch in yellow gold, made in 1993, with off-centre dial indicating the lunar phase. The second hand is located at six o'clock and the power reserve is between ten and eleven o'clock.

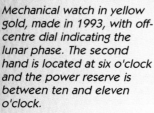

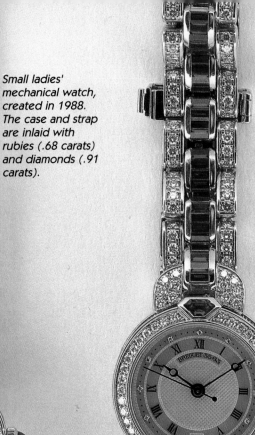

Small ladies' mechanical watch, created in 1988. The case and strap are inlaid with rubies (.68 carats) and diamonds (.91 carats).

Automatic watch from the 1992 Haute Joaillerie collection, with gold case and strap inlaid with rubies (6.80 carats) and diamonds (3.90 carats).

Medium mechanical model in white gold, with bezel, attachments and clasp inlaid with diamonds and sapphires. Made in 1986.

Medium-sized automatic watch from the 1992 Haute Joaillerie collection, with gold casing and strap inlaid with rubies and diamonds.

Ladies' mechanical watch, 1988, with bezel, attachments and clasp in gold, encrusted with 1.60 carats of diamond. The gold chain strap is classic Breguet.

Automatic ladies' watch, similar in style to the models pictured in the top right hand corner of the preceding page, but with emeralds instead of rubies.

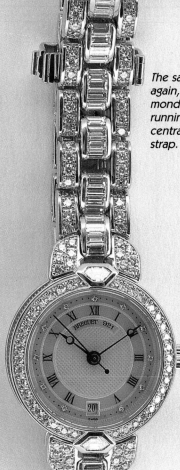

The same model again, but with diamond baguettes running down each central link of the strap.

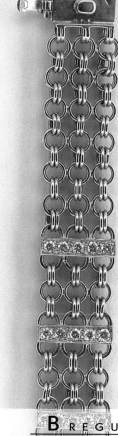

CLASSIC DRESS WATCHES

Medium-sized ladies' mechanical gold watch created in 1986. The bezel, attachments and clasp are inlaid with diamonds and emeralds.

Small ladies' gold watch with bezel, attachments and clasp inlaid with diamonds. 1987.

Mechanical watch with gold bezel and strap decorated with diamonds (1.65 carats) and sapphires (1.35 carats). 1986.

PIONEER OF THE SKIES

Breitling has always played an important role in aviation history, from the first flights through the "jet age" to the first steps on the moon. By perfecting revolutionary techniques, this prestigious watchmaker has in fact achieved its own conquest of space. It was founded in 1884 by Léon Breitling. He died thirty years later, just as the chronograph-strap was born. His son, Gaston, and later his grandson, Willy, took up the torch, and Breitling soon became one of the world's leading watchmakers. By 1936, numerous aviation companies had equipped their fleets with the chronograph designed by Willy Breitling in the Twenties. In 1941, it was Willy who had the idea of fitting the famed timepiece with a circular slide rule. Then in 1952, the Navitimer model appeared, generating a small revolution in the market. But Breitling's finest hour came when, on 24 May 1962, the American astronaut Scott Carpenter wore a new-generation Navitimer aboard the Aurora-7. The pioneers of the skies had hurdled the barrier between time and space. The company moved to Grenchen, and in 1970 it was bought up by the industrial magnate and pilot Ernest Schneider. In 1984, a new Chronomat was unveiled. It had been produced in a limited, numbered series, to celebrate their centenary. This was also the year that Breitling, which had traditionally sponsored the world aerobatics championship, took an interest in sailing and football, and went on to add the Americas Cup and the 1990 World Cup in Italy to their sponsorship list. The most remarkable watches among the latest Breitling "gems" are the Duograph, the Astromat Longitude chronograph, and the Navitimer 92, not forgetting, of course, the exquisite automatic platinum chronometer. The great pioneers of the skies have become veterans of success and quality.

Launched in 1952, the Old Navitimer – pictured here with a steel case – is the recommended watch for aeroplane pilots, and is Breitling's most legendary model. Equipped with a chronograph and a type-52 slide rule, it is an indispensable on-board instrument, used to determine the rate of ascent and descent, fuel consumption, average speed, mile/kilometre conversion, and can even tackle problems such as change conversion.

The Navitimer Avi harks back to the spirit of the 1950s. Made in 1993, this automatic 33-calibre chronograph is a sports Navitimer without slide rule which takes us out of the propeller era and into the age of the reaction engine. It features a bidirectional twelve-hour graduated bezel and a sapphire watchglass. Waterproof to 95 feet.

The 1993 Navitimer Airborne features the shortest hour and minute totalizer which has been deliberately limited to ten minutes. This chronograph is equipped with a Breitling 33-calibre movement, and the readability of its dials is exceptional. It features a calendar with hands, a type-52 slide rule, automatic rewind and a two-sided anti-reflection crystal. Waterproof to 95 feet.

THE NEW PILOTS

1952 Old Navitimer. This automatic model with steel case features a 1/5 second chronograph, 30-minute and twelve-hour dials and a sapphire anti-reflection watchglass. Waterproof to 95 feet, with certified double-gasket crown.

Gold and steel 30-calibre automatic Navitimer 92, with gold and wiredrawn steel strap, complete with type-42 slide rule, tele-meter and pulsometer. It is waterproof to 95 feet. This is Breitling's smallest pilot's model.

This 1991 Shark automatic chronograph features a Breitling 13-calibre movement. Built to last, it is equipped with a large crown protector and ergonomic push-pieces partially set into the case, and a sunken crystal. Waterproof to 325 feet.

This 1992 Breitling 53-calibre Shark quartz chronograph has a rapid time zone change function, a split-second chronograph and a battery life indicator.

With its type-52 slide rule, its 1/50-second chronograph and built-in alarm, the Jupiter Pilot electronic quartz chronograph is equipped to respond to a pilot's demands. Fitted with a Breitling 59-calibre movement, this watch is waterproof to 325 feet. It can be attached to a leather or metal strap.

Launched in 1992, the 57-calibre Breitling Colt is available with either an automatic movement or, as shown here, an electronic quartz movement with battery-life indicator. This watch is the most robust of the Breitling models. It is waterproof to 975 feet with a screwed crown, sunken crystal and raised indexes on the bezel. The hands and numbers are luminescent.

The highly precise Pluton quartz electronic chronograph, launched in 1993, was originally designed for military pilots. It features a combined display, both analogic and digital, as well as a second time zone function and an hourly signal. It also functions as an alarm clock and has a lighted display and compass card bezel.

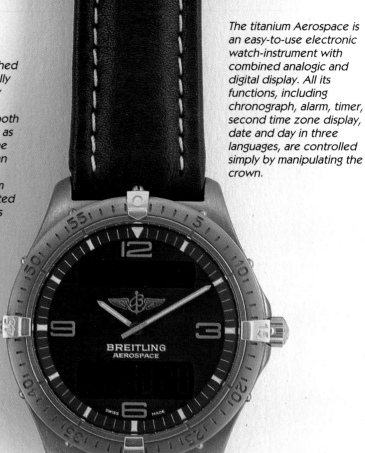

The titanium Aerospace is an easy-to-use electronic watch-instrument with combined analogic and digital display. All its functions, including chronograph, alarm, timer, second time zone display, date and day in three languages, are controlled simply by manipulating the crown.

THE PROFESSIONALS

The Breitling 56-calibre Chrono-space, created in 1992, is a chronograph, timer and alarm, and is fitted with an electronic quartz movement. It was specially designed for Mirage pilots and features a simplified slide rule and a weights and measures conversion scale. It is water-proof to 325 feet. Its electronic functions are similar to those of the Aerospace and they are equally accurate.

The Breitling 56-calibre titanium Aerospace with electronic quartz movement features a numeric display that measures time to 1/100 of a second. The readability of the dial is exceptional aided by the anti-reflection sapphire crystal. Waterproof to 325 feet, with Bol battery-life indicator.

In 1994, this Breitling 13-calibre mechanical Chronomat with automatic winding mechanism was given a new, white dial. The Arabic numerals on the face, protected by an anti-reflection sapphire crystal, are unparalleled in their readability. This model is attached to a leather strap, but can also be attached to roller or Pilot straps.

This mechanical Chronomat with unidirectional notched bezel in gold and steel and automatic winding mechanism ,was created in 1984 for the Frecce Tricolori, the elite Italian Air Force fighter patrol. Its dial features a tachometric scale and its thick sapphire crystal is treated to prevent reflection on both sides, allowing for rapid reading at any angle. Waterproof to 325 feet.

The unusual feature of this mechanical Chronomat with automatic winding mechanism, white dial and small black dials, is its ability to accommodate a second watch set to a different time zone on its steel strap.

This Breitling 13-calibre mechanical Chronomat with automatic winding mechanism is fitted with a blue dial, under a double anti-reflection sapphire crystal. Its steel Pilot strap has a security clasp. Its functions are identical to those of the other Chronomat models.

This chronometer in gold and steel features the Breitling eagle engraved in gold on the dial. It is one of only 1,994 watches that were produced in the Anniversaire series and is a much sought-after collector's item.

THE CHRONOLINERS

The Breitling 55-calibre Chrono Sextant electronic quartz watch, 1989 model, is equipped with a mechanical chronograph to 1/100 of a second, 30-minute and twelve-hour dials, unidirectional bezel and a double anti-reflection sapphire crystal. Waterproof to 325 feet.

...unched in 1992, this Breitling 30-calibre mechanical Chrono ...ckpit with automatic ...ing mechanism has a ...d bezel and indexes ...steel. It is equipped ...with a highly precise miniaturized ...nograph movement. The date display is ...cated between four ...and five o'clock. It is ...terproof to 325 feet ...an be attached to a ...sharkskin leather or metal strap.

This Chrono Cockpit model features a white dial with small blue dials under a double anti-reflection sapphire crystal. Its unidirectional steel bezel has four indexes in 18-carat gold. Waterproof to 325 feet. Shown here on a leather strap.

The 1989 Lady J electronic Breitling 52-calibre quartz model has an elegant yet sturdy design. The case is waterproof to 650 feet, with screwed crown, scratchproof anti-reflection sapphire crystal and battery-life indicator.

Sturdiness, longevity and class are the defining characteristics of this ladies' Callistino quartz watch with electronic movement, created in 1989. Made of gold and steel, this Breitling 52-calibre model with double-sealed screwed crown is waterproof to 325 feet. Its roller strap is in gold and steel.

This steel Callistino features the same technical specifications as the model shown left. The roller strap has been replaced with one in saddle-stitched leather.

Power, finesse and elegance are the hallmarks of this 1994 electronic quartz Callisto, designed with distinctive Roman numerals. The screwed crown is double-sealed. Here it is attached to a Pilot strap, but it can also be worn with a leather or roller strap.

This model in gold and steel, from the Sirius Lady Perpétuel series, is attached to a Pilot-style strap also in gold and steel. It is also available in steel with an enamelled dial. Once properly set, this watch never needs adjusting. Its calendar is programmed to track the days precisely until the year 2100.

Another version of the Sirius Lady Perpétuel, from the Breitling dress watch collection. The case is yellow gold and the diamond-encrusted bezel has four emerald indexes. This watch is programmed to the year 2100.

NIGHT FLIGHTS

This diamond-inlaid 1993 Sirius Lady Perpétuel is from the Breitling dress watch collection. As with all the other Sirius Perpétuel models, the electronic movement of this Breitling 62-calibre model with mother-of-pearl dial, was designed to indicate the exact date until 1 March 2100.

This diamond Callistino dress watch, attached to a Pilot strap also in diamond-encrusted gold, features a mother-of-pearl dial with diamond indexes.

This Lady J Breitling 52-calibre quartz model has a gold case and strap. The dial and bezel are blue and it is waterproof to 325 feet. It is also available with a roller strap.

THE AMBASSADOR OF LUXURY

The international reputation and high esteem in which Cartier is held today is due to the exquisite and timeless designs of such great lines as the Santos and Tank series, both of which have inspired cult-like followings. Today, the Panthère, Pasha and Must collections carry the same cachet and continue to appeal to men and women the world over. Founded by Louis-François Cartier in 1847, it wasn't until 1898, when Louis-Joseph Cartier joined his father's business, that the illustrious jeweller really developed its watchmaking division. Then in 1907, Cartier began to work in partnership with Edmond Jaeger and the two men successfully predicted that strap-watches would soon be all the rage. In 1906, when the Brazilian pilot Alberto Santos-Dumont took to the skies in his first airborne adventures, he wore a Cartier watch. The Santos model would propel Cartier into the upper echelons of watchmaking. Inspired by the American armoured vehicles which took part in the First World War, the Tank, launched in 1919, was another phenomenal success and reinforced the company's growing reputation. With shops in Paris, London and New York, the company now run by the three Cartier brothers had become an international empire. The Vendôme and Tortue were the most coveted watches of the Twenties and Thirties. Then in 1942, following the deaths of his brothers, Pierre Cartier took over. By fitting his watches with movements created by the biggest names in watchmaking, such as Patek Philippe, Vacheron Constantin and Audemars Piguet, he created an image of exclusivity. In 1973, when Robert Hocq was appointed president of the company, Cartier struck another coup with the arrival of the Must collection. In the Eighties, the legendary Tank, Vendôme, Santos and Tortue models were relaunched, all fitted with either mechanical or quartz Cartier movements. Not one to sit on its laurels, the company came up with the superb 18-carat gold Pasha with perpetual calendar: its reputation as a great ambassador of luxury and quality is certainly well deserved.

This Mini-Baignoire watch from the Louis Cartier collection is a reproduction of the original 1920 model.

The curved quartz Santos, in steel and gold with a strap made of small steel plates held together with tiny gold screws, is waterproof to 95 feet. The first model in the Santos line was created in 1978.

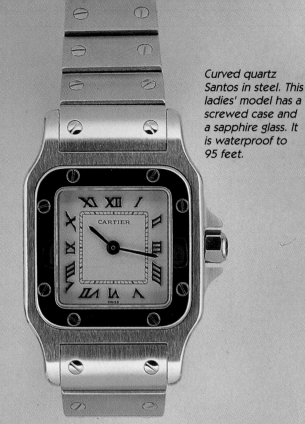

Curved quartz Santos in steel. This ladies' model has a screwed case and a sapphire glass. It is waterproof to 95 feet.

MINI-BAIGNOIRE
AND SANTOS

This round Santos is a new model fitted with an automatic movement. The case and the strap are steel and the white dial has Roman numerals.

Santos ladies' steel model with a 17-jewel automatic movement. The perimeter of the dial and the screws are 18-carat gold. Waterproof to 95 feet.

This sterling silver Must de Cartier which appeared in 1976 is based on an Art Deco design. It has a quartz movement, a crystal watchglass and Roman numerals.

The Must de Cartier Tank watch, in vermeil with a quartz movement. The ivory dial with Roman numerals is protected by a crystal watchglass. Shown here with brown crocodile strap.

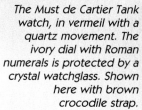

Another Must, this men's model 21 was made in 1986. It has a quartz movement and is mounted on the customary polished 'rice grain' bracelet. As on the ladies' model, the winding button is crowned with a spinel.

Must in vermeil with quartz movement and date display at three o'clock. Shown here on a gold-grained calfskin strap with folding clasp.

This 1986 quartz Must model 21 is mounted on a 'rice grain' strap. The winding button is decorated with a spinel and Roman numerals are engraved on the bezel.

Another version of the model 21, created in 1986. It is presented here on a blue sharkskin strap with a folding clasp. The blue Roman numerals match the colour of the strap.

THE MUST COL-
LECTION

This Must Colisée quartz watch features an ivory dial, crystal watchglass and crocodile strap. This model was created in 1976.

This quartz Vendôme watch in vermeil, created in 1976, is from the Must collection. It comes attached to a gold crocodile bracelet with an Ardillon buckle. A crystal watchglass protects the ivory dial which features Roman numerals.

This Must Tank watch in vermeil features a 1920s dial displaying a double row of Roman numerals which excludes VI and XII. This model is attached to a crocodile strap and is not waterproof.

The Cougar quartz watch, created in 1989. The case, bezel and strap are in brushed stainless steel. The date display is situated at three o'clock and it has a sapphire crystal. Waterproof to 95 feet.

Created in 1994, the ladies' Cougar features a case and bracelet in polished gold (total weight: 4 oz.) and a blue lacuqer dial. It is fitted with a quartz movement.

The Cougar quartz watch in gold (weight: 0.4 oz) and steel with screwed back. Waterproof to 95 feet.

This Cougar watch in brushed stainless steel features a "black sun" dial. The date display is located at three o'clock.

The Cougar ladies' steel model with quartz movement, mounted on a polished steel strap. Waterproof to 95 feet.

The Cougar in gold and steel with 'rice grain' strap with a folding clasp. The date display is at three o'clock.

The white gold Colisée watch from the dress watch collection is mounted on a bracelet made of white gold 'pearls'. The bezel is inlaid with 43 diamonds and the winding button is also crowned with a diamond.

The 1991 Colisée quartz watch with gold case and strap. This is one of the Cartier's most successful models.

COUGAR, PANTHÈRE AND COLISÉE

This gold Panthère watch, first created in 1983, is one of the world's most famous time-pieces. In 1914, Cartier created a watch with a diamond panther, which would later become the company emblem. The model shown here contains 2.2 oz of 18-carat gold.

This line of Panthère watches was first launched in 1985. It comes in three sizes all available in different versions: solid gold, solid steel or jewelled. This model in gold and steel has a quartz movement and is attached to a strap with a double row of gold links.

Men's Panthère quartz model in gold and stainless steel with screwed back. Waterproof to 95 feet.

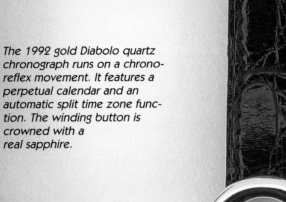

The 1992 gold Diabolo quartz chronograph runs on a chronoreflex movement. It features a perpetual calendar and an automatic split time zone function. The winding button is crowned with a real sapphire.

This Baignoire gold watch from the Louis Cartier collection is a reproduction of the original 1920 model. It has a quartz movement and the winding button is fitted with a sapphire.

The gold Cougar watch has a quartz chronoreflex movement. The dial is white with Roman numerals and the crocodile strap is fitted with an 18-carat gold Ardillon buckle.

This Cougar has a quartz chronoreflex movement. The case weighs 1.1 oz. The watch is also available with a white dial.

The Colisée quartz watch with 18-carat gold case. The winding button is decorated with a small sapphire and the strap is fastened with a gold Ardillon buckle.

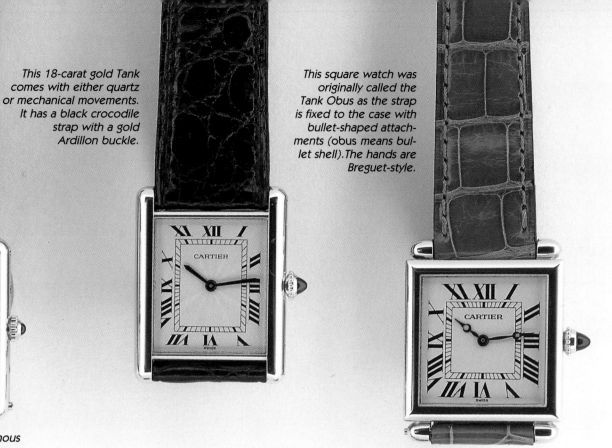

This 18-carat gold Tank comes with either quartz or mechanical movements. It has a black crocodile strap with a gold Ardillon buckle.

This square watch was originally called the Tank Obus as the strap is fixed to the case with bullet-shaped attachments (obus means bullet shell).The hands are Breguet-style.

The Tank is the most famous of all Cartier wristwatches. Designed by Louis Cartier in 1919, it was inspired by the shape of the armoured tanks used in the First World War. This ladies' Tank in 18-carat gold features a 081.8-calibre quartz movement.

COUGAR, TANK
AND DIABOLO

The gold Vendôme watch from the Louis Cartier collection boasts an 18-jewel mechanical movement and a case containing 0.8 oz of gold.

The Diabolo ladies' quartz watch in gold. Both the attachments and the winding button are decorated with sapphire cabochons. It is also available with an 18-carat gold strap.

Pasha watches were the first waterproof timepieces manufactured by the house of Cartier. The first one was created in 1933 for the Pasha of Marrakesh. This 18-carat gold model with a rotating bezel and chased dial is fitted with an automatic winding, 22-jewel mechanical movement. Its total gold weight is 2.5 oz.

Steel chronograph with quartz movement, waterproof to 95 feet. The three totalizer dials are inscribed in white on the champagne-coloured dial. The bezel is unidirectional.

All Pasha watches feature a sapphire cabochon fixed to the winding button, which can be unscrewed to reset the watch. This system was devised to render the watch watertight.

This Pasha watch is 1.48 inches in diameter and has a 22-jewel mechanical movement which winds automatically. It is waterproof to 325 feet.

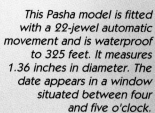

This Pasha model is fitted with a 22-jewel automatic movement and is waterproof to 325 feet. It measures 1.36 inches in diameter. The date appears in a window situated between four and five o'clock.

This split-second steel chronograph with chronoreflex movement has a perpetual quartz calendar. It is waterproof to 95 feet and is attached to a steel strap with a folding clasp.

PASHA WATCHES

This little chronograph is 1.36 inches in diameter, has a chronoreflex movement and a screwed back. The blue crocodile strap matches the colour of the dial.

Steel quartz chronograph, measuring 1.48 inches in diameter. The date display is located at six o'clock, inside the second dial. The hands and indexes are luminescent and the bezel is unidirectional.

HAMILTON
AMERICA'S FINEST HOUR

Hamilton watches, originally produced for the railway pioneers towards the end of the 19th century, have witnessed some of the seminal events of American history. From the conquest of the Wild West to Hollywood's conquest of Europe, Hamilton has assumed its rightful place in the American Dream. It all began in 1892 in Lancaster, Pennsylvania, when five men, John Brimmer, Peter Watt, Charles Rood, Harry Cochran and George Franklin, founded the Hamilton Watch Company, named after Andrew Hamilton, the district attorney who fought tirelessly for freedom of the press. The first Hamilton produced was a pocket watch designed by the engineer Henry J. Cain for locomotive conductors. At the time, Hamilton's main rivals were Waltham, Elgin, Aurora, Illinois and The American Watch and Clock Company. In 1922, Hamilton launched an advertising campaign with a poster depicting a train running at full steam across which ran the slogan: "The watch of the 20th century". In 1928, Colonel Jacob Ruppert, the owner of the World Series champion baseball team, commissioned a commemorative watch from Hamilton. Legendary players such as Babe Ruth and Lou Gehrig were each presented with an extraordinary Piping Rock Yankee watch with their team emblem engraved on the underside of the case. During the Second World War, Hamilton was the official supplier of marine chronometers to the Navy. The company also supplied aviation chronographs and navigation equipment to the Air Force and made watches for the GIs. After the war, Hamilton unveiled three great models: the Spectra, Ventura and Van Horn. In the Sixties, film director Stanley Kubrick commissioned a watch and a futurist clock from Hamilton for his film *2001: A Space Odyssey*, while the Seventies saw the arrival of technology inherited from Japan, in the form of the digital display Pulsar. Today a whole new generation of watch lovers is being seduced by quartz remakes of classic Hamilton designs from the Forties and Fifties. The American Dream lives on.

This Hamilton mechanical chronograph from the Piping Rock Yankee series is a reissue of the 1938 model. The case is plated in white gold, with Roman numerals engraved on the bezel. It is equipped with 30-minute and twelve-hour totalizers. The glass is in Plexiglas and the strap is lizard skin.

Automatic steel chronograph fitted with a unidirectional bezel. The watchglass is crystal and the date display at three o'clock is overlaid with a loupe for easy reading. This watch also features three totalizer dials with a small second hand located at twelve o'clock.

This Hamilton quartz watch from the Benton series is a 10-micron gold-plated reproduction of the 1930 model. It features a Plexiglas crystal, Arabic numerals and a second hand dial at six o'clock.

PIPING ROCK YANKEE

This handsome piece is also a remake of the 1930 model. The case is beautifully curved and the dial inscribed with Arabic numerals is copper. A small second hand is located at six o'clock and the watchglass is made of crystal.

Piping Rock Yankee watch with quartz movement. It features a 10-micron gold plate case, a second hand dial located at six o'clock, a Plexiglas crystal and lizard strap.

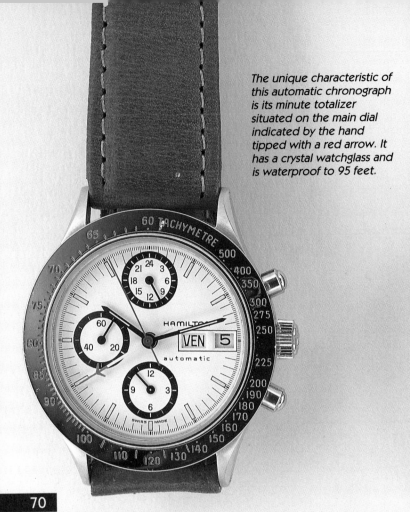

The unique characteristic of this automatic chronograph is its minute totalizer situated on the main dial indicated by the hand tipped with a red arrow. It has a crystal watchglass and is waterproof to 95 feet.

This quartz sports model is waterproof to 650 feet. It comes with a screwed winding button and unidirectional bezel. The sharkskin strap matches the dial.

This elegant little chronograph is a reproduction of a 1930s model. It features a guilloche bezel and crystal watchglass, three dials located at three, six and nine o'clock and a lizard strap.

This steel quartz chronograph is accurate to 1/10 of a second. The date window is situated at six o'clock, overlapping the minute dial. It has a unidirectional bezel, a crystal watchglass and a steel strap. Waterproof to 95 feet.

Automatic steel chronograph with a fixed bezel featuring a tachometric scale. A loupe at three o'clock on the sapphire crystal enhances date readability. Waterproof to 95 feet.

The "Fiftieth Anniversary" watch was produced in association with Khaki, to commemorate the Normandy Landings. It is an exact replica of the same watch worn by the GIs who landed on the beaches of northern France. The case is engraved with the insignias of all four American armed forces. This model is fitted with a quartz movement and is waterproof to 95 feet. It comes attached to a woven strap.

COMMEMORATIVE REPRODUCTIONS AND NEW QUARTZ WATCHES

This Hamilton Khaki quartz model is cased in shot-peened steel. The hands are luminescent, as are the hour indexes. It is waterproof to 95 feet and shown here on a leather strap.

This quartz model is one in a series created in honour of the Airborne Special Forces army corps. The matt black case was specially designed so as not to reflect the moon. The black dial is protected by a sapphire crystal. Waterproof to 325 feet.

This Piping Rock Yankee mechanical chronograph has the same technical specifications as the model shown on page 68.

This mechanical watch in white gold is a reissue of the piece presented to each member of the baseball team that won the 1928 American championships.

This Ventura is a 1957 reproduction of an electronic model originally designed by Hamilton in 1950. This was the first battery-run, mechanical movement timepiece. Triangular in shape and made of rose gold, it is now fitted with a quartz movement. The black dial is covered by a Plexiglas crystal.

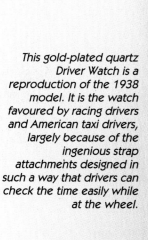

This gold-plated quartz Driver Watch is a reproduction of the 1938 model. It is the watch favoured by racing drivers and American taxi drivers, largely because of the ingenious strap attachments designed in such a way that drivers can check the time easily while at the wheel.

This 10-micron gold-plated reproduction of a 1960 model features a transparent back which reveals the automatic movement.

An updated quartz version of a 1960 Hamilton model. The bezel is decorated with a double gadroon. As with many Hamiltons, this model is gold-plated.

The gold-plated Benton watch, with second hand at six o'clock, is also available with a gold-plated stretch strap. The watchglass is crystal and it is waterproof to 95 feet.

Piping Rock Yankee watch in quartz with a black Bakelite bezel and black dial. It has a Plexiglas crystal and a second hand at six o'clock.

FROM THE VENTURA
TO THE DRIVER

Barrel-shaped Hamilton ladies' watch, in 10-micron gold plate with quartz movement and crystal watchglass. Shown here with a leather strap.

A classic rectangular gold-plated Hamilton for men, with a second hand at six o'clock, a quartz movement and a lizard strap.

IWC

THE SCHAFFHOUSE DESTRIER

I t all began in 1869, when Florentine-Aristo Jones, a master watchmaker from Boston, was lured to Schaffhouse by a local businessman. Following a damaging investigation into trade tariffs, Jones returned to the United States in 1876 and The International Watch Company (IWC) was then bought by Schaffhauser Handelsbank. Later, a businessman by the name of Johannes Rauschenbach-Vogel decided to turn the American business into a purely Swiss concern, a policy later pursued by the Homberger family and the VDO group, which acquired the company in 1978. IWC had established its reputation back in 1893 with the invention of the calibre 52, later known as the Schaffhouse calibre. It has specialized in the creation of complicated movements ever since, reaching its peak with the pocket watch version of the Grande Complication. The "Probus Scafusia" stamp became an unrivalled mark of quality, prized by serious collectors – Tsar Ferdinand of Bulgaria, Pope Pius IX and Winston Churchill all wore IWC watches. Despite its quotation on the American market, however, IWC struggled through a financially difficult period from the Wall Street Crash in 1929 until after the War. But the launch of the double-cased pendulum watch in the Fifties marked a turning point. Twenty years later, an agreement was drawn up between IWC and Porsche, which resulted in several successful Porsche designs, including the Ocean 2000. During the 'quartz revolution', IWC continued to design such complicated models as the Da Vinci. Then in 1990, the Grande Complication was born, followed in 1993 by IWC's flagship model, the Schaffhouse Destrier, launched to mark its 120th anniversary. This was succeded by the Portugieser Uhr, a commemorative limited edition comprising 1,000 models in steel, 500 in red gold and 125 in platinum – IWC has come a long way since the first Jones movement.

The Schaffhouse Destrier is the unparalleled masterpiece of watchmaking. To commemorate IWC's 120th anniversary, 125 of these mechanical models in rose gold were produced. The watch is composed of 750 mechanical gear works which perform a total of 21 functions including a split-second chronometer with fly-back hand, a lunar phase display and a perpetual calendar which indicates the date, year, decade and century.

The first watch in the Da Vinci series was created in 1985. This 39-jewel mechanical chronograph with automatic winding mechanism beats at a frequency of 28,800 vibrations per hour, and comes in white, yellow or rose gold as well as in steel. It features a perpetual calendar with lunar phase indication and screwed crown. It is waterproof to 95 feet.

This Da Vinci model with 18-carat gold case and strap features the same technical specifications as the model to the left. Note the four-figure year display located between seven and eight o'clock. Every one hundred years, a gear advances the century indicator by 1.2 millimetres.

The gold Portofino (reference 3541), with perpetual calendar and lunar phase display, contains an automatic movement which beats at a frequency of 28,800 vibrations per hour. Protected by a sapphire crystal the main dial features three small day, date and month dials. The year is indicated in the small display located between seven and eight o'clock. It is waterproof to 95 feet.

IWC didn't begin to produce its Da Vinci series in steel until 1992. For the first seven years of its life, the model came only in gold or ceramic. This steel model has exactly the same technical specifications as the other Da Vinci models.

The Novecento made its debut in 1987. It is one of the few rectangular timepieces which has a mechanical movement with automatic winding mechanism. It is made of yellow gold and has a black or white dial which indicates lunar phase, year and decade. It is waterproof to 95 feet.

Chronograph with titanium case and strap, automatically winding mechanical movement and a frequency of 28,800 vibrations per hour. Fitted with 25 jewels and a sapphire crystal, this piece is waterproof to 195 feet.

The gold and titanium Ocean 500 is a diver's watch fitted with an automatic winding mechanical movement. It features a screwed crown, date display, and a second hand with a stop function. It also exists in pure titanium.

The Reiseuhr titanium traveller's watch also comes in a gold and titanium version. Its original feature is the indicator which displays the time in 21 different countries. It also has an alarm function and is waterproof to 95 feet.

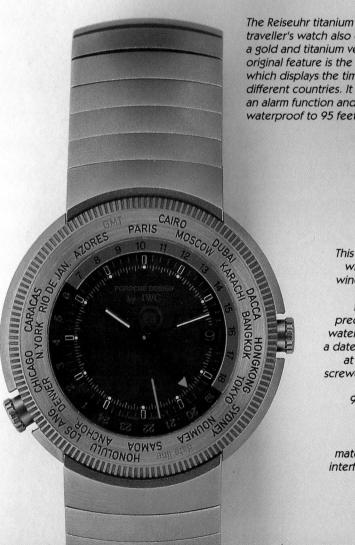

This watch-compass with an automatic winding mechanical movement also features a highly precise, detachable waterproof compass, a date display located at three o'clock, a screwed crown and is waterproof to 95 feet. All these timepieces are produced with paramagnetic materials to prevent interference with the compass.

The Lady Titane shown here in polished titanium also exists with a gold and titanium bezel. This quartz model features a date display and sapphire crystal. Waterproof to 195 feet.

Unlike the Lady Titane, the Titane model for men has a mechanical movement with an automatic winding mechanism. It is also comes with a black dial and is available in a gold and titanium version. Waterproof to 195 feet.

PORSCHE DESIGN
BY IWC

The Sportive 02 is a small mechanical chronograph in gold measuring 1.17 inches in diameter. It runs on a quartz-driven stepping motor, and is fitted with a date display and a screwed crown. It is waterproof to 95 feet and is also available in a steel version.

This stainless steel Sportive 01 quartz watch features a date display and second hand with a stop mechanism, and a battery-life indicator. Waterproof to 95 feet.

The steel Flieger chronograph is the smallest chronograph in the world featuring an analogic display. All its functions are driven by two stepping motors and are controlled via two push-pieces. An inner case of soft iron protects the movement from magnetic fields. Its sapphire crystal resists the effects of depressurization. Waterproof to 95 feet.

The Portofino chronograph in stainless steel is 1.17 inches in diameter and is thought to be one of the thinnest watches in the world. Its mechanical movement is driven by quartz stepping motors. It is waterproof to 95 feet and has a sapphire crystal. This piece is also available in gold.

Superb 18-carat gold version of the small Da Vinci chronograph with lunar phase display.

Ingénieur gold and steel Chrono Alarm on a steel strap, with mechanical chronograph movement and alarm function. Driven by two quartz stepping motors, this watch has a screwed crown, sapphire crystal and is antimagnetic to 4,800 A/m. Waterproof to 95 feet.

The 18-carat gold prestige model of the Fliegerchronograph is attached to a crocodile strap with a gold Ardillon clasp. It has the same technical specifications as the steel Flieger pictured opposite.

This gold Da Vinci ladies' chronograph is 1.13 inches in diameter and features a mechanical movement with quartz stepping motors. Its enamelled dial features a perpetual lunar phase indicator and it has a screwed crown and sapphire crystal. Waterproof to 95 feet.

is 1992 steel Da Vinci model with ar phase display features all the same technical specifications as e other Da Vinci odels illustrated in this chapter.

The Doppelchronograph is a mechanical chronograph with an automatic winding mechanism. It features a split-second function and indicates the day and date in the display located at three o'clock. It has a screwed crown and an inner case of soft iron to shield the movement from magnetic fields.

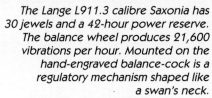

The Lange L911.3 calibre Saxonia has 30 jewels and a 42-hour power reserve. The balance wheel produces 21,600 vibrations per hour. Mounted on the hand-engraved balance-cock is a regulatory mechanism shaped like a swan's neck.

The Lange 1 features an L901.0-calibre movement. Fitted with 53 jewels, it is regulated in five positions. The double barrel accommodates a power reserve which can exceed three days.

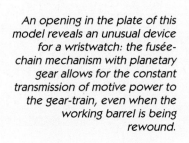

An opening in the plate of this model reveals an unusual device for a wristwatch: the fusée-chain mechanism with planetary gear allows for the constant transmission of motive power to the gear-train, even when the working barrel is being rewound.

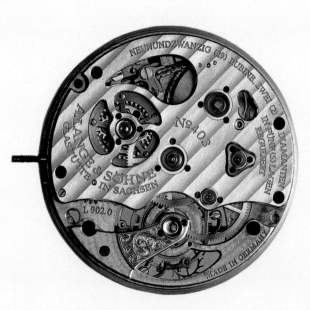

The Merit, named after the most prestigious honour awarded in Germany until 1918, is a pretty rare timepiece: only 150 gold and 50 platinum watches were produced. This model has a visible tourbillon and planetary gear, and the second and the power reserve dials are situated at nine and three o'clock. It is dedicated to the company founder, Ferdinand Adolph Lange.

The mechanical Saxonia wristwatch in gold, with screwed bezel and case back. The sterling silver dial features a date display located at twelve o'clock and the second dial is at six o'clock. It is attached to a crocodile strap with a gold buckle.

The Arkade ladies' mechanical wristwatch, in gold. Its design was inspired by the arcades in the courtyard of Dresden castle. A date display is located at twelve o'clock on the sterling silver dial and the screwed back case is in 18-carat gold. The strap, shown here in crocodile with a gold buckle, also comes in a handmade solid gold version. This model also exists without the second hand at six o'clock.

This gold Lange 1 wristwatch features a mechanical, double barrel movement. The main dial is off-centre, the second dial is located at five o'clock and the power reserve indicator is at three o'clock. The date appears in a dual display situated at twelve o'clock.

JAEGER-LeCOULTRE
THE REVERSO LEGEND

In 1833, Charles-Antoine Le Coultre founded his own watchmaking company and went on to create timepieces with revolutionary calibres and complex movements. Nearly a century later, his grandson, Jacques-David Le Coultre, forged a partnership with Edmond Jaeger. Jaeger had great respect for the company and had chosen LeCoultre movements for Cartier watches. Six years after they went into partnership, the two men launched the exceptional timepiece which was to epitomize their great skill. It was in their watchworks in the small town of Sentier, nestling in the Jura mountains, that one of the most legendary wristwatches ever made was born: the Reverso. Designed in 1931 by René-Alfred Chauvot and produced by Jaeger-LeCoultre, it was originally intended specifically for polo players. Its innovative flip-around face was designed to protect the watch face from damage during play. Who would have thought that this pivotal design would become one of the most famous watches of all time? Jaeger-LeCoultre and Reverso are synonymous, though the firm has put its signature to many other distinguished models, such as the Duoplan, the Atmos clock, the Futurematic and the superb Memovox – a beautiful alarm watch and the predecessor of the Grand Reveil and the Chronograph alarm. Jaeger-LeCoultre has stepped into the Nineties with two exceptional timepieces: Master Control and Géographique, on top of which they released a limited, numbered edition of 500 new dual-faced watches to mark the sixtieth anniversary of the Reverso (1931-1991). Every element of the watch's case and movement is made out of rose gold and its heart can be seen beating through a transparent sapphire crystal back. The great Art Deco masterpiece has not aged a bit in its sixty or so years of existence. It is an exceptional timepiece that transcends both the whims of fashion and time itself.

This Memovox alarm watch, which comes in both gold and steel, is an early 1960s design. It is a unique masterpiece with an automatic movement and a mechanical alarm. The alarm is regulated by the winding button located at two o'clock and the small arrow found along the inner rim of the dial. The back of the case is perforated which makes for a rather loud wake-up call.

Dubbed the "two-faced watch", this prestigious steel Duoface Reverso is from the 1994 collection. The case pivots on itself within the square base fixed to the leather strap. This remarkable mechanical model indicates two time zones on two different dials, each is independent of the other but both are driven by the same movement.

JAEGER-LECOULTRE
THE REVERSOS

The Reverso was created in 1931 especially for polo players. The dial of this 1992 Reverso Shadow is the work of Deleskiewitch, a French watchmaker of Polish origin. It is made of brushed and polished steel and attached to a metal strap.

This Duoface model was designed in 1994 and features two time zone displays driven by the same movement: the Jaeger-LeCoultre calibre 854. The small dial functions as a 24-hour display to track the hour in the country of reference.

JAEGER-LECOULTRE
THE REVERSOS

This Reverso in rose gold is the reproduction of a 1950s model fitted with a mechanical movement. The Reverso design underwent a number of changes between 1975 and 1985, most notably the elimination of decorative elements on the surface of the supporting plate which appears when the watch is reversed.

This steel Reverso is a faithful reproduction of the original model designed in 1931. It exists today with either a quartz or a mechanical movement. Back in 1931, advertisements for the Reverso focused on the protective qualities of its reversible face, targetting those who played sports or engaged in manual activities.

Since 1931, the Reverso has been a great Art Deco classic, as this ladies' quartz Reverso so perfectly illustrates. It features a gold case, sapphire crystal and ostrich leather strap.

The 24-hour side of this watch has a gold guilloche case, a chased sterling silver dial and an ostrich leather strap. This is one of the most remarkable models Jaeger-Le Coultre have ever designed. It is such exquisite timepieces as this one which have earned them the reputation of outstanding watchmakers.

This yellow gold Reverso with matching strap is sheer perfection. The steel hands have been 'blued', a process by which steel is tempered in a furnace. The casing is certified 'hand finished'.

This steel Reverso features a wonderful portrait, engraved by Christophe Parat, of Antoine Le Coultre, who founded the company in 1833. But it is to Jacques-David Le Coultre, Edmond Jaeger, César de Trey and René-Alfred Chauvot that we owe the Reverso.

Ladies' Reverso, with steel case and strap. This particular strap was made at the watchworks and assembled entirely by hand. The ladies' Reversos have "faces" as varied as those on the Reversos designed for men.

The Géographique, first presented in 1990 at Switzerland's Foire de Bâle, is the dream watch for travellers. This new model can tell the time in two cities simultaneously with the window located at twelve o'clock, which includes all the major cities around the world, and the dial at six o'clock, which can be set to the relevant local time.

This ultra-thin gold Odysseus ladies' chronograph features a lunar phase display and the smallest complete chronograph movement in the world. It is one-third the size of the classic chronograph movement, which was designed in 1989 for the larger chronograph with lunar phase display.

This men's Odysseus gold chronograph with lunar phase display tracks leap years in the day, month and year displays. The strap is also made of gold.

JAEGER-LECOULTRE

THE MASTERPIECES

Steel version of the Heraion chronograph. This watch has a movement which comprises 300 hand-assembled pieces, and has seven indications: hours; continual minutes; hours, minutes and quarter of a second in chronograph function; wake-up time and date. It is also available in a solid gold and in a steel and gold version.

The Odysseus has simple day/date with lunar phase and day/month/date displays which are regulated by the push-pieces incorporated into the case. This gold model has a sapphire crystal and is attached to an ostrich leather strap.

The Jaeger-LeCoultre Grand Reveil with lunar phase display is a perpetual day calendar with alarm function. The alarm bell is made of a special bronze alloy which was perfected in China around 1500 BC.

The ultra-thin Heraion watch is equipped with a combined mechanical and quartz movement. But its most original feature lies in its ability to measure the wearer's heartbeat using a scale located on the bezel. This model is also available in gold.

In 1931, Reverso adopted the slogan, "The Reverso is magical: turn it once and it's a watch, turn it twice and it's a bracelet!". In the case of this Reverso Tourbillon, the real magic lies in the mechanism. Its mechanical movement achieves the greatest precision thanks to its tourbillon balance, invented by Abraham-Louis Breguet at the end of the 18th century.

The legendary Géographique mechanical watch, launched in 1992, indicates the time in two cities simultaneously. The names of 24 capital cities as well as their local times appear on a disc driven by micro-peens. Waterproof to 160 feet, this watch also features a power reserve indicator.

The Master Control with steel case and strap undergoes 1,000 hours of inspection in the manufacturer's workshop. A numbered certificate is delivered with each one, and on the underside of the case a gold lozenge bears the watch's individual number.

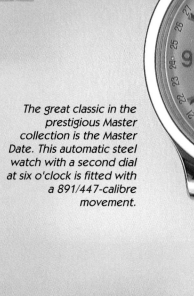

The great classic in the prestigious Master collection is the Master Date. This automatic steel watch with a second dial at six o'clock is fitted with a 891/447-calibre movement.

The automatic Master Reveil is the latest model in the Master collection. Its winding button is located at two o'clock and controls the alarm function as well as the internal dial indications.

This 889/1-calibre automatic Master Control is fitted with a magnetic steel case and a 21-carat gold rotor. It is waterproof to 260 feet. A crocodile strap enhances its classic appeal.

The Master Date in gold has an identification number on its case. Waterproof to 260 feet, it has a sapphire crystal and a crocodile strap.

The ultra-thin mechanical Master in gold is fitted with a sapphire crystal and has a frequency of 28,600 vibrations per hour. It is also available in steel.

The 34-jewel Master Date has a hand-assembled movement composed of 300 parts. It is waterproof to 260 feet.

THE MASTERS

This automatic Master Control with gold case and folding clasp was part of the 1992 Jaeger-LeCoultre series and it boasts a frequency of 28,600 vibrations per hour. The signature and date of inspection are engraved inside the case by the master watchmaker Michel Rochat.

Another version of the Master Control, which master watchmaker Michel Rochat tested under extreme vibration and temperature conditions. It comes with a certificate of authenticity and a production number.

Manufactured in the 1950s, the mechanical Memovox has a Plexiglas crystal, a steel case and a screwed back. This model is a landmark in the history of Jaeger-LeCoultre.

This Etrier ladies' model was manufactured by Jaeger-LeCoultre for Hermès. The shape echoes the highly successful Arceau watch by Hermès.

JAEGER-LECOULTRE

THE EARLY MODELS

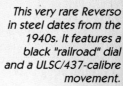

1930s ladies' dress watch by Jaeger-LeCoultre with a two-tone dial, Arabic numerals and a double leather cord.

1930s Jaeger-LeCoultre ladies' dress watch, with mechanical movement and a woven double cord.

This very rare Reverso in steel dates from the 1940s. It features a black "railroad" dial and a ULSC/437-calibre movement.

This 1930s Duoplan model is driven by a superimposed two-level mechanism. It does not have a winding button, but is set from underneath by a fluted roller.

Gold and steel wristwatch with lunar phase display in a "date case", created specially for Cartier in 1945. Quartz reproductions of this model are available today.

With its Art Deco case and black dial, this 1920s Duoplan was a veritable technical revolution in its day. Two 11 BF 409-calibre movements are superimposed in keeping with its diminutive size. The Duoplan technical patent dates from 1926.

Ladies' Jaeger-LeCoultre in steel, made in 1948, with 8 NR/496-calibre mechanical movement, attached to a leather strap.

Yellow gold pocket watch made in 1900 with rose-coloured dial and a small second dial at six o'clock.

LONGINES

ADVENTURE AND DISCOVERY

On 21 May 1927, at precisely 22:22, the Spirit of Saint Louis piloted by Charles Lindbergh landed at Le Bourget landing field in Paris after a flight lasting 33 hours and 30 minutes. This historic moment was officially timed by Longines and marked the beginning of a collaboration between the American colonel and his watchmakers. In that same year Lindbergh himself designed a watch for use as a navigation instrument, which he commissioned from his friend, the director of Longine's New York division. This timepiece was destined to change pilots' lives the world over. It was designed to indicate the hour, horary angle, equation of time and to synchronize with radio signals. Lindbergh's preliminary sketches evolved into the Angle Horaire chronographs, which are struck with a winged hourglass, now the company logo. Two years later, commander Philipp Van Horn Weems, an officer of the US Navy at the Naval Academy of Annapolis where Charles Lindbergh had been a student, registered a patent for an invention which was simple and decisive: it enabled watches to be synchronized to the second with radio signals, using the exterior lunette or the central dial, as both were graduated and could rotate. Inspired by this discovery, Longines created the Weems Pilot Watch. In the world of sport, Longines fought long and hard against its rival Omega and began to specialize in the official timing of automobile races. The 1988 Formula 1 chronograph, from the Conquest collection, is still considered the model of reference. In 1989, to celebrate its centenary, Longines unveiled a highly complicated watch called Effemeridi Solari, or the "astronomic automatic" model. Other prestigious chronographs and watches soon followed, including 100 platinum models of the chronograph and the Cristobal C made in commemoration of Columbus and the discovery of America.

This gold and steel chronograph from the Angle Horaire collection was manufactured by Longines in honour of the great aviator, Charles Lindbergh. It is based on a model which Lindbergh designed himself in 1927, for his solo Atlantic crossing. This watch is used by professional aviators: it calculates the horary angle and the equation of time, and features a radio signal synchronization function. The day and date indicators are situated in two displays located at three o'clock. The movement is visible through the transparent back.

This Lindbergh Angle Horaire watch is a historic reproduction of the original model worn by the aviator, with automatic movement, steel case and gold bezel. The back opens to reveal the movement as well as a commemorative inscription. The buckle on the strap is a reproduction of the 1930s design.

CITY WATCHES

This model is a re-edition of a 1930s Longines design, with automatic movement, Arabic numerals, Plexiglas crystal, date display, central second hand and steel case. It is waterproof to 95 feet.

A quartz Conquest in steel and gold plate, attached to a steel and gold-plated strap. It is equipped with a date display located at three o'clock and a battery-life indicator. This Conquest is waterproof to 325 feet and also exists with a white dial.

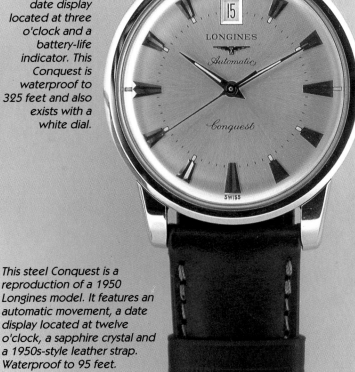

This steel Conquest is a reproduction of a 1950 Longines model. It features an automatic movement, a date display located at twelve o'clock, a sapphire crystal and a 1950s-style leather strap. Waterproof to 95 feet.

This steel watch from the Conquest collection is attached to a steel strap which fastens with a folding clasp. It has a sapphire crystal, a date display at three o'clock and is waterproof to 325 feet.

This elegant ladies' quartz Conquest model is gold plated. Waterproof to 95 feet, it features a date display at three o'clock, a sapphire crystal and a battery-life indicator.

This gold and titanium Conquest is fitted with a perpetual calendar which keeps track of 28, 29, 30 and 31 day months, and is programmed to the year 2100.

This Conquest in gold plate and steel is fitted with an automatic movement that is visible through its transparent case. This watch is certified waterproof to a depth of 325 feet.

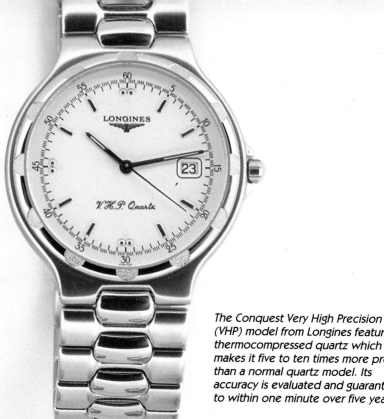

This silver and gold plate ladies' Conquest features the same technical specifications as the model shown on the left.

The Conquest Very High Precision (VHP) model from Longines features thermocompressed quartz which makes it five to ten times more precise than a normal quartz model. Its accuracy is evaluated and guaranteed to within one minute over five years.

THE CONQUESTS

The quartz Conquest model with case and strap in gold plate and steel is fitted with a folding clasp and sapphire crystal. The date display is located at three o'clock. Waterproof to 325 feet.

This quartz Conquest with case and strap in gold plate and steel is shown here with a white face. It features the same technical specifications as the model shown opposite.

This gold automatic watch is from the 1833 Ernest Francillon collection, which was named after the nephew of one of the company founders.

This automatic Pionnier model was turned out in a limited edition of 3,000 steel and 1,500 gold and silver models and only 500 numbered pieces in solid gold. It can tell the time in 21 countries around the world.

This mechanical watch is a reproduction of a 1930s model. It has a Curvex barrel-shaped case and a small second dial located at six o'clock.

Automatic watch in yellow gold from the Ernest Francillon collection. This watch is fitted with a central second hand and features a date display located at three o'clock.

This automatic watch in yellow gold from the Ernest Francillon collection is fitted with a back that opens to reveal the movement. It has both lunar phase and date indicator.

This mechanical chronograph in yellow gold from the Ernest Francillon collection has a particularly exquisite case and a first-rate movement.

THE FRANCILLON, ADMIRAL AND CONQUEST COLLECTIONS

This quartz chronograph, which is accurate to 1/10 of a second, is part of the Conquest collection. The case and the strap are in stainless steel and it is waterproof to 325 feet.

This automatic chronograph with tachometric bezel is part of the Admiral collection. It also exists with a white face attached to a leather strap.

OMEGA
WALKING ON THE MOON

At the turn of the century, traditional watchmaker Louis Brandt & Frère changed its name to Omega, a company which, in April 1970, received the highest distinction bestowed by NASA, the Snoopy award. Never has a success story been so meteoric. From hot air balloon races, to the conquest of space, to the Olympic Games, the Brandt family has always run ahead of the pack. When in 1894 César and Louis Brandt produced their first pocket watch equipped with a 19-line calibre, they could not have foreseen that by the dawn of the next century their annual production would exceed 200,000 watches: an industrial-scale output which in no way detracts from the quality of an Omega watch. The business was handed down from father to son and from 1917 onwards the new winning Brandt quartet (Adrien, Paul, Gustave and Ernest) invested in aviation, and Omega soon became the favoured make among American and British aviators alike. Omega's own conquest of space began in 1965, when NASA decided to equip its astronauts with the Speedmaster chronograph. On 21 July 1969, when Neil Armstrong and Edwin "Buzz" Aldrin made their historic walk on the moon, Omega was there too. Since that memorable day, Speedmaster Professional chronographs have participated in all the American space programmes, from Gemini through Apollo to the Shuttle. Around this time, Omega was chosen by the International Olympic Committee to be the official timer of the Olympic Games, a task it would accomplish on more than 20 occasions with resounding success. After reaching outer space and the Olympic stadiums, Omega set out to sea and produced the Seamasters that have descended with deep sea divers to depths of 1600 feet. The company has also created watches with prestige complications, such as the Louis Brandt models, which are manufactured in numbered limited editions, while Omega's greatest success to date is still the Constellation watch.

When American astronaut Neil Armstrong stepped onto the moon and checked the time, it was an Omega Speedmaster Professional strapped to his wrist. This Speedmaster automatic chronograph in gold with triple day/month/date calendar, is a masterpiece of watchmaking. The date is indicated by the hand with the small black crescent moon.

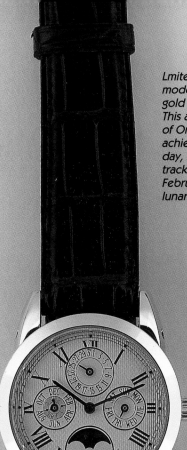

Lmited edition Louis Brandt model featuring an 18-carat gold case and gold clasp. This automatic watch is one of Omega's proudest achievements. It indicates the day, month and date and tracks 30-day months, 28 February, leap years and lunar phases.

This gold and steel Speedmaster automatic chronograph does not feature a date display. The chronograph dials are located at three, six and nine o'clock. It has a sapphire crystal, champagne-coloured dial and leather strap, and is waterproof to 95 feet: very good value for money.

SPEEDMASTER AND SEAMASTER

Omega created two limited editions of the Seamaster: one for the 1988 Olympic Games in Seoul and the other for the 1992 Games in Barcelona. This Seamaster in gold and steel, with a gold and steel strap, comes fitted with either a quartz or an automatic movement. It is waterproof to 390 feet and also exists with blue, black or champagne-coloured dials.

This Speedmaster chronograph in gold and steel features a small 24-hour dial located at nine o'clock. It is fitted with a sapphire crystal and a crocodile strap. Waterproof to 95 feet.

This gold Speedmaster chronograph has a frequency of 28,600 vibrations per hour and features a day/month/date display and a sapphire crystal. Waterproof to 95 feet. This model also exists with a blue dial and a gold and steel strap.

The distinctive feature of all models in the Seamaster collection is the special screwed back designed to make the watch water-resistant to a depth of 390 feet. This model with steel strap comes with both quartz and automatic movements.

This Seamaster, with gold and steel case and strap, is also available in a gold version. It is a certified (observatory-tested) chronograph equipped with a security clasp for divers. Waterproof to 390 feet.

This unique Seamaster chronograph in titanium, tantalum and gold is waterproof to 975 feet. Designed for deep sea diving, it features push-pieces and a winding button located at ten o'clock which functions with a helium valve.

This Speedmaster automatic chronograph with steel case is also available with a large white dial and small black dials. It features a rapid date setting function, a sapphire crystal and is waterproof to 95 feet.

The Seamaster automatic in gold and steel with blue dial, luminescent indexes, enamelled dial and sapphire crystal. Waterproof to 390 feet.

SPEEDMASTER AND SEAMASTER

This Seamaster ladies' model in gold and steel features a screwed crown and back and is guaranteed waterproof to 390 feet. This model with a blue dial and luminescent indexes also comes with a white or champagne-coloured dial.

This splendid steel Speedmaster chronograph features a day/month/date display. Fitted with a sapphire crystal, it is waterproof to 95 feet and is also available with a cream-coloured dial. The strap is made of matt Louisiana crocodile.

This Omega is interesting for its 1950s-style barrel shape. It has a quartz movement and the white dial features Roman numerals. It is attached to a crocodile strap.

This gold and steel ladies' quartz watch is from the De Ville collection. It has a sapphire crystal and a date display located at three o'clock. Waterproof to 95 feet.

Ladies' watch in gold with champagne-coloured dial from the De Ville collection. It features the same technical specifications as the previous model. It is fitted with a crocodile strap and gold-plated buckle.

Another watch from the De Ville ladies' collection, with 18-carat gold case, date display located at three o'clock, central second hand, sapphire crystal and crocodile strap.

This gold and steel De Ville men's watch features a date display at three o'clock and a central second hand. A champagne-coloured dial is protected by a sapphire crystal. This model is also available with a blue, white or cream dial on a gold and steel strap.

The De Ville quartz watch for men. The sapphire crystal protects a white dial with Roman numerals. This model is of a minimalist design and features neither a date display nor a central second hand.

Men's gold quartz watch with square case and gold strap. The dial is white with Roman numerals, protected by a sapphire crystal.

The legendary Constellation model is the pride of Omega. This men's watch in gold and steel is distinctive for the Roman numerals inscribed along the circumference of the bezel. Features include a battery-life indicator and a sapphire crystal. Waterproof to 95 feet.

THE DE VILLE RANGE

Omega men's watch from the De Ville collection, in gold and steel. This model features a date display located at three o'clock and a sapphire crystal. It has a cream dial and a crocodile leather strap.

The famous ladies' version of the Omega Constellation. The case and strap are in gold and steel, but this model also exists in solid 18-carat gold. This watch is one of Omega's most successful models.

Omega ladies' model from the De Ville collection with case and strap in gold and steel. Under the sapphire crystal is a champagne-coloured dial with a date display located at three o'clock. Waterproof to 95 feet.

PATEK PHILIPPE

A LEGEND AMONG WATCHMAKERS

Six years after Antoine-Norbert de Patek and François Czapek set up the watchmaking business Patek, Czapek & Co in Geneva in 1839, Adrien Philippe, who had just revolutionized the industry by perfecting the first watch which could be rewound without a key, stepped into Czapek's shoes. In 1851, Patek Philippe & Co was established, and in 1889 sold a watch to Queen Victoria at the first Universal Exhibition in Paris. Between 1845 and 1991, the company registered twelve major patents. Tradition, innovation and uncompromising quality are the key to Patek Philippe's international success. For over 150 years, the company has combined the seven elements indispensable to the art of fine watchmaking, blending to perfection the skills of stylist, watchmaker, goldsmith, chain- maker, engraver, enamellist and jeweller. But Patek Philippe also prides itself on mastering the profession's supreme aptitude test – the complicated timepiece. One of their finest designs has to be the 89-calibre movement pocket watch, which features 33 complications and represents the invest-ment of all of Patek Philippe's expertise and experience in the art.

Since it was established, Patek Philippe has produced only 600,000 watches, but all of its models have transcended time and fashion. The legendary Calatrava, which is more than 60 years old, remains one of their most popular models, while the Ellipse, though it has been around for nearly thirty years, never seems to date. In 1932, the year in which the Stern family assumed control, Patek Philippe created the most complicated timepiece ever produced for American collector and magnate Henry Graves Junior. Exceptional watches require exceptional anniversaries, and to celebrate 150 years in the industry the Geneva-based manufacturer launched the complicated minute repetition model with perpetual calendar, alongside the jumping hour model. In 1992, Patek Philippe again succeeded in surprising the market with a barrel-shaped watch complete with minute repetition, perpetual calendar and retrograde day/date: a work of art decorated with the Calatrava cross, the company emblem.

This magnificent yellow gold Montre Tonneau (literally barrel-shaped watch) for men was first presented by Patek Philippe at the 1992 Foire de Bâle. Its functions are multiple: minute repetition, lunar phase display, perpetual calendar and retrograde day/date.

The Calibre 89 in gold by Patek Philippe remains the most complicated watch ever produced. It is a pocket watch with two dials and 33 complications and comprises 1,728 pieces, 24 hands and eight discs. First begun in 1980, the Calibre 89 wasn't completed until nine years later, in time for the company's 150th anniversary. It weighs 2.4 pounds and gives full expression to the three principle types of complication: the calendar, chronograph and striking mechanism.

THE LEGEN-DARY CALIBRE 89

Patek Philippe in yellow gold with a calendar which tracks leap years. It features an automatic movement and indicates the lunar phase. 1992 model, reference 5040.

Automatic watch In yellow gold, with perpetual calendar. Its retrograde calendar hand is a new, highly precise mechanism perfected by Patek Philippe. 1993, reference 5050.

Rose gold watch, featuring an automatic movement and perpetual calendar with lunar phase indication which tracks leap years. Attached to a black crocodile strap. 1985, reference 3940.

This Patek Philippe watch in yellow gold indicates the age and phase of the moon. It is fitted with a power reserve indicator and a sapphire crystal. 1993, reference 5015.

The Patek Philippe model is a superb chronograph in rose gold with a manual winding mechanism. It is fitted with a 30-minute dial and a perpetual calendar with lunar phase display. Ideal for travellers, it also gives am/pm indications. 1986, reference 3970.

COMPLICATED
WATCHES

This mechanical chronograph in yellow gold indicates the lunar phase and may be regulated to the minute for the lunar year. It has a perpetual day/date calendar and also indicates am/pm. 1994, reference 5020.

The classic automatic Calatrava 3998, which is considered to be the perfect example of Patek Philippe's great craftsmanship.

This Calatrava 3820 in rose gold with Breguet-style hands and Arabic numerals runs on an ultra-thin mechanical movement.

The Calatrava 3998/1, with yellow gold case and strap. This automatic watch with central second hand and date display located at three o'clock illustrates the diversity of style in Patek Philippe' timepieces.

Extremely rare Calatrava 3883 skeleton model in yellow gold with ultra-thin mechanical movement. More than sixty years after its first appearance, this series is still one of Patek Philippe's greatest success stories.

The Calatrava series was named after the Calatrava cross that the house of Patek Philippe adopted as its emblem. Reference 3802/200 is an automatic watch in yellow gold with central second hand and date display.

The Calatrava 3796 in rose gold features a mechanical movement. A sapphire crystal protects the rose gold dial which has a small second hand located at six o'clock.

This Calatrava mechanical model in rose gold (reference 3919) with leaf-shaped hands, Roman numerals, porcelain dial and leather strap is the one that the Patek Philippe chose to represent the company image.

Reference 3796 D is another famous timepiece. It is also a mechanical watch, but is made in yellow gold and has a small second hand located at six o'clock.

Patek Philippe named this model the Gondolo in reference to the Gondolo chronometers produced around the turn of the century for the Brazilian company Gondolo & Labourian. This 5014 model in gold is fitted with a mechanical movement.

This Gondolo model was inspired by 1930s Art Deco style. It features a mechanical movement and Arabic numerals and is also available in yellow gold. 1993, reference 5014.

The unique, delicately curved shape of the case on this watch requires an extremely exacting manufacturing technique. This model in rose gold is fitted with an ultra-thin mechanical movement, reference 3842.

This exquisite mechanical Gondolo (reference 5010/1) with case and strap in yellow gold features a sapphire crystal, porcelain dial, Roman numerals and a small second hand located at six o'clock. It encapsulates all the elements of Patek Philippe 1990s design.

The skeleton Ellipse (reference 3880) in yellow gold has an ultra-thin mechanical movement and is one of the most original and coveted Patek Philippe models. Already over a quarter of a century old, this is a line that will never date.

To keep the Ellipse d'Or well out of the counterfeiter's reach, Patek Philippe designed an ingenious 18-carat gold dial with a blue face and automatic movement (reference 3738/100). The gold hands and indexes look as if they are floating on the sea-blue dial.

GONDOLO AND ELLIPSE

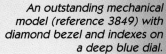

Ellipse with mechanical movement (reference 3978/17), and case and strap in 18-carat yellow gold. A white dial with Roman numerals in black is protected by a sapphire crystal and the second hand is located at six o'clock. The first model in the Ellipse collection was created in 1968.

An outstanding mechanical model (reference 3849) with diamond bezel and indexes on a deep blue dial.

This Nautilus watch in steel is fitted with an automatic movement. The case is enclosed by a rounded octagonal bezel and a hand-cut, specially fitted crystal watchglass. The Nautilus was designed in 1976.

Sculpted from a block of gold, this Nautilus watch with automatic movement is waterproof to 390 feet. The strap and indexes are also in gold. It features a second hand and a date display located at three o'clock.

The Patek Philippe Nautilus in gold and steel features the same technical specifications as the two watches pictured above.

The Nautilus ladies' model in gold is fitted with a quartz movement. The dial features gold indexes, a date display located at three o'clock and is covered by a sapphire crystal. This watch is waterproof to a depth of 195 feet.

This Nautilus ladies' watch in gold and steel features the same technical specifications as the model shown opposite.

THE NAUTILUS COLLECTION

A superb Nautilus from the dress collection, with diamond bezel and indexes.

This Nautilus from the dress collection is very rare. It has a diamond-encrusted strap, bezel and dial and the four indexes are ruby baguettes.

The exquisite 1994 quartz Gondolo watch (reference 4845/11) is wrought from a harmonious blend of yellow gold, diamonds and sapphire baguettes. The diamond indexes are protected by a sapphire crystal.

This unique Ellipse is fitted with a quartz movement. The white gold setting is inlaid with diamonds. It has a sapphire crystal, Arabic numerals, and a mother-of-pearl dial. 1994, reference 4832.

Yellow gold Flamme watch (reference 4816/3) with quartz movement and diamond indexes. The crown and the central part of the strap are also inlaid with diamonds.

This exquisite 1994 quartz Ellipse (reference 4831/11) is made of yellow gold, diamonds and rubies. The mother-of-pearl dial beneath the sapphire glass is inscribed with Arabic numerals.

This classic 1994 Gondolo (reference 4824) features a quartz movement, a yellow gold case and Arabic numerals inscribed on a white dial. This watch is mounted on a traditional leather strap.

This original Gondolo is mounted on a satin strap. The quartz watch in yellow gold and diamonds features diamond indexes. 1994, reference 4825.

LADIES' WATCHES

The quartz Calatrava (reference 4820/1) is an elegant blend of white gold and diamonds. A sapphire crystal protects a white dial with Roman numerals.

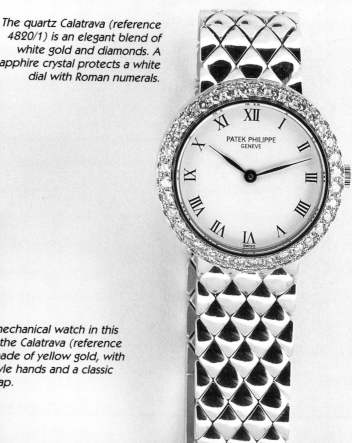

The only mechanical watch in this selection, the Calatrava (reference 4860) is made of yellow gold, with Breguet-style hands and a classic leather strap.

ROLEX
A UNIVERSAL SUCCESS

The saga of the world's most famous name in watches – from the very first waterproof watch, made in 1926, to the "Paul Newman" Oyster Perpetual Cosmograph Daytona – began with a young orphan's passion for the art of watchmaking. In 1905, Hans Wilsdorf, a 24-year-old German who began life in the trade importing and exporting prestigious Swiss watches, founded a company in London called Wilsdorf & Davis. Three years later, this visionary, who was convinced of the future popularity of the wrist watch, registered the Rolex trademark in Switzerland, at La Chaux-de-Fonds. The first Rolex timepiece was presented at Bienne and for fifteen years, Rolex reigned as the epitome of quality and precision. In 1914 and 1915, Wilsdorf timepieces were awarded two Class A Certificates. But the man who would later become a master watchmaker in his own right was hard at work on a very ambitious project: the first waterproof watch. In 1926, Wilsdorf registered the patents for the Rolex Oyster. The resulting wristwatch was put to the test in July 1927, when the swimming champion Mercedes Gleitze wore a Rolex as she swam the English Channel in 15 hours and 15 minutes. When she came ashore, the watch was found to be perfectly intact and functional. From that moment, the rise of Hans Wilsdorf and Rolex was vertiginous, a trajectory strewn with discovery and triumph: in 1931 the Oyster Perpetual and the 360-degree rotor were born; in 1938, the Bubble Back masterpiece was created; then in 1945 came Datejust followed in 1953 by the Submariner, a watch that can withstand a pressure of up to 100 metres. That same year, Sir Edmund Hillary conquered Mount Everest with a Rolex on his wrist. The company entered the Sixties on a high note: one of its models, the Oyster Special, descended to a depth of 35,477 feet below sea level, fitted to the exterior of Jacques Picard's bathyscaph Trieste. In the mid-Seventies, following years of research, Rolex invented what would become the world's favourite chronograph, the legendary Oyster Perpetual Cosmograph Daytona immortalized by Paul Newman.

The Oyster Perpetual Cosmograph Daytona in gold and steel. It was named in honour of the racing drivers who competed on the famous race-track in Florida and who certainly appreciated its instantly readable dial. This Rolex series was designed in 1976 and also exists in solid steel or 18-carat gold. The Daytona collection also includes a "Paul Newman" model, named after the actor who has worn this watch on every international circuit.

Oyster Perpetual Cosmograph Daytona: This 18-carat gold and steel chronograph features a Fliplock security clasp. Made in 1988, this watch is available with a black, white or champagne-coloured dial and diamond indexes. It is waterproof to 325 feet.

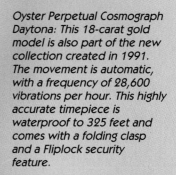

Oyster Perpetual Cosmograph Daytona: This 18-carat gold model is also part of the new collection created in 1991. The movement is automatic, with a frequency of 28,600 vibrations per hour. This highly accurate timepiece is waterproof to 325 feet and comes with a folding clasp and a Fliplock security feature.

Oyster Perpetual Cosmograph Daytona: This steel model belongs to the 1992 series. Shown here with a white dial, it also comes with a black dial. The push-pieces and winding button are screwed to keep the watch waterproof. The sapphire crystal is scratchproof and virtually unbreakable, and the steel strap features a Fliplock security clasp.

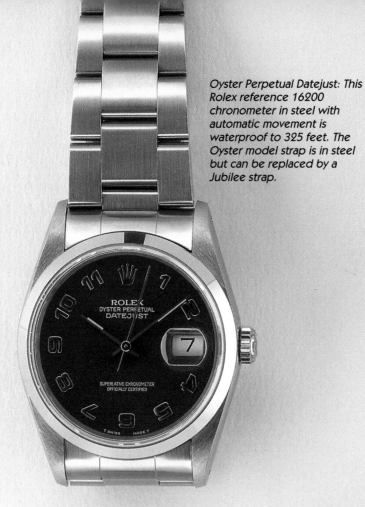

Oyster Perpetual Datejust: This Rolex reference 16200 chronometer in steel with automatic movement is waterproof to 325 feet. The Oyster model strap is in steel but can be replaced by a Jubilee strap.

Oyster Perpetual Datejust Turn-O-Graph: This automatic chronometer in gold and steel has a gold bezel and is waterproof to 325 feet. The gold and steel Oyster strap can be replaced by a Jubilee strap.

Oyster Perpetual Air-King: This automatic watch only exists in steel with an Oyster strap. It has a sapphire crystal and is waterproof to 325 feet.

Oyster Perpetual Explorer II automatic chronometer in steel with Oyster strap. It features a 24-hour bezel and hand. The independently regulated 12-ho hand means the watch can be s to two different time zones.

Oyster Perpetual Date Submariner: This gold and steel chronometer is fitted with a Fliplock security strap. The rotating bezel is graduated to control decompression time. Note the shoulders protecting the crown. This model also comes with a black bezel and gold contouring. Waterproof to 975 feet.

Oyster Perpetual Date Yacht-Master: This model only exists in 18-carat gold with a white dial. Its 60-minute, graduated rotating bezel is designed in relief. Waterproof to 325 feet, with a sapphire crystal and shoulders for protecting the crown.

SPORT WATCHES

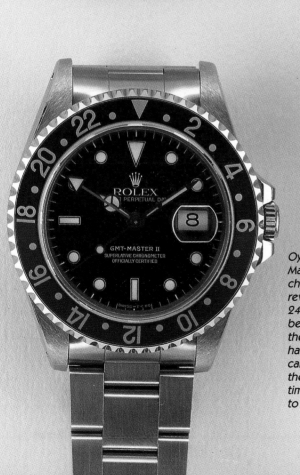

Oyster Perpetual GMT-Master II: This steel chronometer has a revolving two-tone, 24-hour graduated bezel. The addition of the independent red hand means the watch can be set to indicate the time in two different time zones. Waterproof to 325 feet.

Oyster Perpetual Date Submariner: This steel chronometer is equipped with a Fliplock security strap and is waterproof to 975 feet. The revolving bezel is graduated to indicate the level of decompression.

Oyster Perpetual Day-Date Super President: This chronometer exists in 18-carat yellow gold and in white gold. The days are displayed in English, but are also available in 25 other languages. It has diamond indexes, an automatic movement and a sapphire crystal. This is the watch worn by the Pope and is a favourite with Presidents and heads of state.

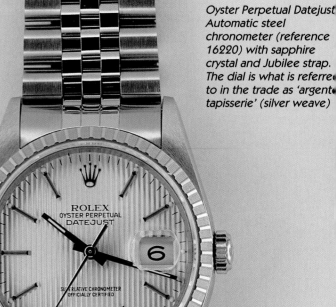

Oyster Perpetual Datejust Automatic steel chronometer (reference 16220) with sapphire crystal and Jubilee strap. The dial is what is referred to in the trade as 'argenté tapisserie' (silver weave)

120

Oyster Perpetual Datejust: This watch and Jubilee strap in gold and steel features an ivory dial with Arabic numerals.

Oyster Perpetual Datejust: This automatic chronometer in gold and steel is available in seventeen different dial designs, seven of which feature diamonds, and is one of the great classics in the "city-sport" range. Waterproof to 325 feet.

Lady Oyster Perpetual: Gold and steel ladies' model, attached to a gold and steel Oyster strap. Its movement is automatic, and it is fitted with a sapphire crystal. Waterproof to 325 feet.

Oyster Perpetual Datejust: This automatic steel chronometer has a white dial with Roman numerals and a sapphire crystal. It is fitted with instant date change function. Waterproof to 325 feet.

Oyster Perpetual Lady Datejust: The most popular ladies' model in the "city-sport" range, this chronometer in gold and steel is shown here with a gold dial inlaid with ten diamonds. There are nineteen dial design options for this model. Its movement is automatic and it is fitted with a sapphire crystal.

Oyster Datejust 31-millimetre (1.2 inch): This intermediary automatic model carries the reference 68240. It is presented here with a Jubilee strap, but also exists with an Oyster strap.

Lady Oyster Perpetual: This model in gold and steel is available in a solid gold version. Shown here with a Jubilee strap, it can also be fitted with a steel and gold Oyster strap. It has an automatic movement and a sapphire crystal.

This Oyster Perpetual Date in steel dates back to the 1960s. It has a Plexiglas crystal and is waterproof to 160 feet.

This Oyster Perpetual Datejust, designed in the mid-1960s, is a certified chronometer, as indicated on the dial. It has a Plexiglas crystal and is attached to a Jubilee strap.

ROLEX
CLASSIC CITY MODELS

This 1960s Turn-O-Graph is a rare model. Its unidirectional bezel is made of white gold, the case and strap are steel and the crystal is Plexiglas. Waterproof to 160 feet.

The mechanical "Shock-Resisting" Oyster was made by Rolex in the 1950s. It has a polished bezel, white dial, enamelled indexes and is attached to a leather strap.

This 1940s Oyster Perpetual is from one of the first waterproof series Rolex made and features a screwed winding mechanism, luminescent numbers and rhodium movement. It is certified with 19 jewels and a monometallic balance. It is attached to a crocodile strap.

Because of its limited distribution, this 1970s quartz model is highly prized. The integrated strap adds to its originality.

This Oyster Date Precision from the mid-1940s is equipped with a mechanical movement. The case and riveted "American style" spring strap are gold-plated.

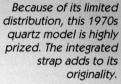

This automatic Oyster Perpetual Bubble Back from the late 1930s is one of the great early Rolex legends. Its steel case is 1.25 inches in diameter and with its innovative bubble-shaped screwed case back it was their first waterproof model.

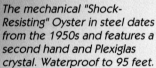

The mechanical Rolex gold Precision dates back to the 1940s. The hours are indicated by the Rolex logo at 12 o'clock, three Arabic numerals and eight intermediary indexes. It is protected by a Plexiglas crystal and attached to an ostrich leather strap.

The mechanical "Shock-Resisting" Oyster in steel dates from the 1950s and features a second hand and Plexiglas crystal. Waterproof to 95 feet.

A typical 1950s design Oyster Date Precision mechanical watch in steel, with screwed winding mechanism, Plexiglas crystal and "American-style" link strap.

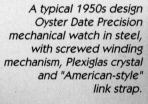

The 1970s Oyster Submariner in steel with date display located, logically, at three o'clock. It has a bidirectional bezel, a Plexiglas crystal with a loupe over the date display, and screwed winding mechanism. Waterproof to 650 feet.

This superb steel model from the late 1920s was the first watch to cross the English Channel on a swimmer's wrist without being damaged. Its bubble back is screwed, as is the winding mechanism.

Oyster mechanical model from the 1950s, in steel with screwed winding mechanism, Plexiglas crystal, Arabic numerals and ostrich leather strap.

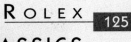
The highly sought after "James Bond" Submariner model was produced in the 1950s. It was named after Sean Connery who wore it in the film Dr No. It has a screwed winding mechanism and is waterproof to 325 feet. Note the luminescent eggshell-coloured indexes.

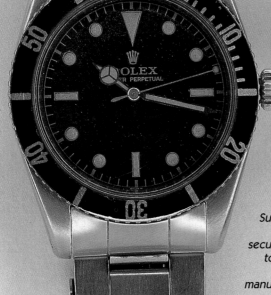

As with the "James Bond" model, this 1970s steel Submariner does not have a date display. It features a security clasp that can expand to fit around a wetsuit. This model is still being manufactured, but with certain technical improvements.

THE FASHION PHENO- MENON

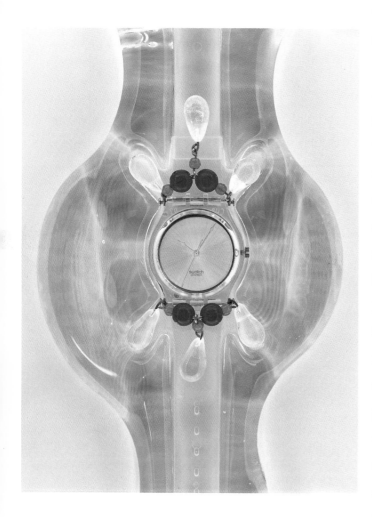

Swatch recently celebrated the sale of its one hundred millionth watch at a memorable party thrown in Zermatt in September 1993 – such a vast amount of watches sold in just ten years is certainly a feat worth celebrating! Swatch has already gone down in history as the watch that revolutionized traditional watchmaking and gave the art a new lease of life. Although there are a few purists who maintain that Swatches are mere gadgets, their voices carry little weight against a vast majority of people worldwide who participated in this revolution. According to legend, the company name is derived from the contraction of the words "Swiss" and "watch". The name Swatch has since become synonymous with innovation, charm and success. Though the triumph of Swatch is largely due to Nicholas Hayek, the president of the SMH group, which conceived, designed and distributed the brand, the original concept resulted from the meeting of two engineers, Jacques Muller and Elmar Mock. Bernard Muller, Jacques's brother, joined the pair along with his companion, the designer Marlyse Schmid. In 1982, the first Swatch appeared on the market. It was as fresh and fun as it was accurate. Weighing just 0.64 oz and waterproof to 95 feet, with a thermoplastic glass, and soldered with ultrasound, the 51-piece quartz mechanism was moulded in ABS plastic. The great appeal of this revolutionary timepiece lay in its price, reliability and the sheer range of different models on offer and above all the highly affordable watches could be matched with any outfit, from the classic and conservative to the outrageous and avant-garde. Because Swatch design was a reflection of the times, it became an instant worldwide success. With a wide range of fashionable designs, it was soon the object of a collecting mania. On 15 August 1990, the company set up The Swatch Collectors of Swatch, a club which quickly spread to the United States, Italy and Japan, as well as the *Swatch Street Journal* stock exchange. Today, the new models, especially the chronographs, are still snatched up ... and there are certainly no signs of the Swatch phenomenon dying out just yet.

This Chandelier Swatch was produced in a limited edition for Christmas 1992 as part of the Swatch Christmas series. It is decorated with Murano pearls and presented in a wooden box.

Left to right:
From the quartz Scuba family (1994), these diving watches with unidirectional bezels are waterproof to 650 feet.

The 1994 Silver Baron belongs to the new generation of Swatches, which are fitted with an automatic movement.

1988 Swatch Scuba model, produced for the 1988 Olympic Games in Seoul.

REFLECTIONS OF AN ERA

A commemorative model, launched in April 1992 to celebrate Swatch's tenth anniversary and the sale of over 100 million watches worldwide.

128

Pompadour
Swatch,
Christmas at
Versailles
model, 1988.

Hollywood
Dream Swatch,
1990.

Asetra
Swatch,
1991.

The classic
Pompadour
Swatch,
1988.

1985 Limelight
model, deco-
rated with
rubies, sap-
phires, eme-
ralds and dia-
monds on the
dial.

Sun King
Swatch,
Christmas
1993 model.

Mozart Swatch,
Christmas in
Vienna model,
1989.

Bergstrüssli
Swatch,
1987.

Peter Früh
Swatch, 1991.

Limelight II Swatch, first marketed in 1987. It was nicknamed "the diamond Swatch".

Test Swatch (1991), designed by Chérif and Sylvie Defraoui. This model celebrates Switzerland's 700th anniversary.

Classic Swatch. The original feature of this model is its transparent, protective double case.

Flack model, produced in 1991 by Nicklaus Troxler, founder and director of the Willisau Jazz Festival, in celebration of Switzerland's 700th anniversary.

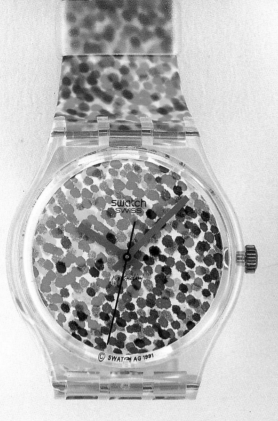

The 360-degree Su Rosso Blackout model, created in 1991 by Italian designer Felice Varini for the 700th anniversary of Switzerland.

Lot of Dots Swatch, created in 1990 by the Milanese architect Alessandro Mendi. This model was presented to each member of the Swatch Collectors Club.

THE COLLECTORS CLUB

Wheel Animal model, created in 1991 by Vital, the Swiss-born New York artist, for the 700th anniversary of Switzerland.

The Swatch "4349" is a rare piece named after the number on the certificate of authenticty presented to this quartz watch-chronometer by the "Controle officiel suisse des chronographs"

TAG HEUER
AVANT-GARDE TECHNIQUE

Ever since Edouard Heuer founded the Swiss company, TAG Heuer's chief domain has been the world of sport. In 1889, at the Universal Exhibition in Paris, Edouard Heuer received his first international prize for his collection of chronographs. But this was only the beginning of a long series of successes. In 1920, sixty years after it was established, Heuer was voted official chronometer for the Antwerp Olympic Games. The Swiss company later took its timepieces to the Olympic Games in Paris, Amsterdam, Moscow and Lake Placid. The inventions and patents followed one another in quick succession and included the Mareograph, the Microtimer, which was precise to 1/1000 of a second, and the Microsplit. The watchmaker soon turned its sights to other games, and Heuer entered the world of the Formula 1 championships from 1971 to 1979, where the highly acclaimed company provided the official chronometers for the Ferrari team. In 1985, the TAG group (Techniques d'Avant-Garde) acquired the majority of shares in TAG Heuer, and in 1992, the International Automobile Federation chose TAG Heuer as the official chronometer for the Formula 1 racing championships. The merger with TAG resulted in a remarkable line of watches called the Sport et Elégance (S/el) series. In 1988, the year the S/el chronograph featuring a 1/10 second dial was created, Carl Lewis signed a contract with TAG Heuer. Ever faster and ever stronger, the 1500 and 4000 series appeared on the market in 1990. The Pilot chronograph is a real multi-function "on-board computer" waterproof to 650 feet. The 1000M watch is waterproof to 3250 feet. With its graduated 24-hour bidirectional bezel and second hour hand, the GMT indicates the hour in two time zones simultaneously. Then, in 1995, TAG Heuer launched a limited series of watches in honour of the late Ayrton Senna. All proceeds from this watch go to the Foundation for Underprivileged Children in Brazil founded by the world motor-racing champion just prior to his tragic accident.

The TAG Heuer 6000 series is the company's most prestigious collection to date. Designed with automatic movement, unidirectional bezel and a date display located at three o'clock, this timepiece is a certified chronometer and is waterproof to 650 feet.

Watch from the S/el series, with quartz movement, unidirectional bezel and screwed winding mechanism. Waterproof to 650 feet, with sapphire crystal and leather strap.

This 2000-series chronometer has a quartz movement, shot-peened steel casing and screwed crown, and is waterproof to 650 feet. A sapphire crystal protects three dials located at two, six and ten o'clock and a date display located at four o'clock.

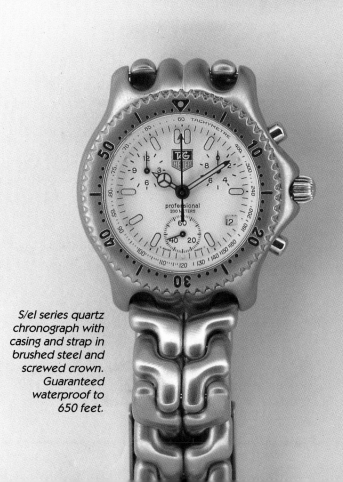

S/el series quartz chronograph with casing and strap in brushed steel and screwed crown. Guaranteed waterproof to 650 feet.

The certified chronometers in the renowned TAG Heuer 6000 series come with either quartz or automatic movement and with silver, grey, blue, black or champagne-coloured dials. The beautifully designed case exists in solid gold or gold and steel.

This chronograph 2000 with quartz movement is waterproof to 650 feet and features luminescent hands and indexes, 1/10 second dial and split-time display. It is available with a leather strap, as shown here, or attached to a shot-peened steel strap. This particular model features black dials on a grey face.

The minute totalizer on this quartz chronograph 2000 is inscribed on the main dial. The 1/10 second totalizer is located at two o'clock, the second hand at six o'clock, the date display at four o'clock and the hour dial at ten o'clock.

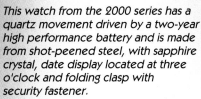

This watch from the S/el Leather series features an automatic quartz movement, a leather strap with folding clasp, a battery-life indicator and a date display located at three o'clock. It is also available in a gold and steel version with a white dial. Waterproof to 650 feet.

This watch from the 2000 series has a quartz movement driven by a two-year high performance battery and is made from shot-peened steel, with sapphire crystal, date display located at three o'clock and folding clasp with security fastener.

Another chronograph 2000, with automatic movement, shown here in gold and steel on a leather strap. It features a screwed winding mechanism and a loupe over the date display for instant readability. Waterproof to 650 feet.

Quartz watch from the S/el series with a steel and gold plate case, and luminescent hands and indexes. Waterproof to 650 feet.

THE 2000
AND S/EL SERIES

Medium S/el Leather model with quartz movement, steel case and grey dial, unidirectional bezel, screwed winding mechanism and battery-life indicator. Waterproof to 650 feet with saddle-stitched water buffalo leather strap.

Medium quartz model from the S/el Leather series, with case in steel and gold plate. It features the same technical specifications as the models shown above.

Quartz S/el model, presented on a polished and brushed steel strap with security clasp. The hands and indexes are luminescent, and the watch features a battery-life indicator.

This quartz S/el model also comes with an automatic movement. It has a grey dial with a date display located at three o'clock, and with its screwed unidirectional bezel and push-piece this model is guaranteed waterproof to 650 feet.

Ladies' S/el model, with steel case and strap, quartz movement and screwed unidirectional bezel and push-piece, making it waterproof to 650 feet.

S/el chronograph with quartz movement, shown here with white dial, steel case and brushed steel strap, two small dials and date display situated at four o'clock.

Medium S/el model, featuring the same technical specifications as the ladies' model pictured left.

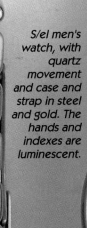

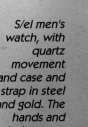

Steel chronograph with quartz movement, accurate to 1/10 of a second. It has a minute totalizer and a date display located at four o'clock. This model is also waterproof to 650 feet.

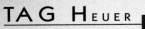

TAG HEUER 137

S/EL SPORT AND SOPHISTICATION

From the S/el ladies' series, this beautiful quartz model features a gold-plated case and strap and luminescent hands and indexes.

S/el men's watch with gold-plated bezel and winding mechanism and brushed steel strap. It features the same technical specifications as the other S/el models.

Ladies' version of the same S/el model, with case and strap in gold plate and steel.

ZENITH
EL PRIMERO

By the time Switzerland celebrated its 700th anniversary in 1991, Zenith, founded by Georges Favre-Jacot at Locle, in the Swiss canton of Neufchatel, was already 126 years old. In a fitting celebration for this double anniversary, Zenith launched a double limited series of its most prestigious chronograph, the peerless El Primero.

This distinguished watchmaking company has won hundreds of prizes, awards, gold medals and records all certified by the world's most famous observatories. Some claim that, to date, it has received no less than 1,500 distinctions. At the start of the 20th century, Zenith had already gained a reputation for the quality of its chronographs. Its renown was international, establishing the brand across Europe and in America. Its marine chronometers figure among the best in Swiss manufacture. For the master watchmakers at Zenith, tradition does not stand in the way of innovation and research – with the El Primero chronographs, Zenith was on the cutting edge of technology. This revolutionary automatic movement, which oscillates at a frequency of 36,000 vibrations per hour, has a 50-hour reserve minimum and is even used by its competitors. The first models in the El Primero series appeared in 1969. Research began in 1966 and was continued until 1989 to perfect the "ultimate" chronograph which reached its apogee with the famous limited edition of 1991. The following year, Zenith expanded the El Primero family by introducing yet another prestigious and beautifully designed chronograph: the Rainbow, a superb sports watch named after the American sloop that beat Endeavour to defend the 15th Americas Cup at Newport in 1934. The limited edition of 500 automatic chronographs produced for Zenith's 125th anniversary were also equipped with El Primero calibres. In 1993, the Locle-based manufacturer created another innovative timepiece, the quartz Via Veneto, which embodied both the art and the carefree charm of the Italian lifestyle.

The El Primero is one of the great landmarks in watchmaking. This 1993 gold-plated El Primero chronograph with lunar phase indicator features the best movement in the world. It is one of the few pieces to run on a column wheel, the basis of all true chronograph movements. It has a 410-calibre automatic movement with a frequency of 36,000 vibrations per hour and features an enamelled dial with three day/month/date displays.

This variation on the standard El Primero has a 410-calibre movement and several complications, including a lunar phase indicator and three day/month/date displays, as on the model pictured opposite.

The El Primero chronograph with tachometric scale is considered as a symbol of Swiss watch manufacture at its best. This model is easily identified by the distinctive logo engraved on the crown and the date display situated at four o'clock.

THE EL PRIMERO CHRONOGRAPHES

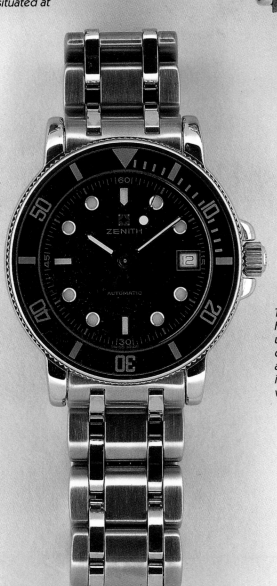

This El Primero diver's model has an automatic movement, unidirectional bezel, screwed crown and comes attached to a steel strap. The hands and index are luminescent and it is waterproof to 650 feet.

This 1994 chronograph in 18-carat gold features rectangular push-pieces. The date display is situated inside the silver dial between four and five o'clock. The case is attached to a gold ostrich leather strap with gold buckle.

This automatic chronograph is a rare piece. It was produced in a limited series of 900 to commemorate the 700th anniversary of Switzerland. The certified chronometer is numbered on the dial and on the back of the case, and it features gold push-pieces, hands and indexes.

This Rainbow 400-calibre El Primero automatic chronograph first appeared in 1992. It has a power reserve of over 50 hours, chronograph functions, and 30-minute and 12-hour totalizers. It also features start/stop and reset push-pieces. Watch functions include hours, minutes, seconds, calendar, instant date change and rapid date reset.

Classic Prime watch-chronograph with manual winding mechanism, launched in 1994. The movement is visible through a transparent back. It has a black dial with luminescent hands and numbers, rectangular push-pieces and a date display located between four and five o'clock.

This automatic Rainbow chronograph is fitted with an El Primero 400-calibre movement and features the same functions as the model shown on the page opposite, bottom left.

Launched in 1992, this El Primero diver's watch has an automatic Zenith movement, screwed crown and push-pieces and a unidirectional bezel. It is mounted on a steel and gold strap and is waterproof to 650 feet.

This gold El Primero automatic chronograph on a crocodile strap has a bezel with tachometric scale to complement its other timekeeping functions. It also features an anti-reflecting sapphire crystal.

INDEX

GLOSSARY

Ardillon: The mobile, pointed part of a buckle which pierces the leather strap when the watch is fastened.

Balance: The oscillating part of the watch which regularizes the force of the wheelworks and includes a mainspring. Certain makes, such as Patek Philippe and Rolex, have patented balances.

Battery: The driving force of a quartz watch.

Cabochon: An unfaceted, polished precious gemstone used to decorated the dial or the crown of a watch.

Calendar: Revolving discs which indicate the succession of days, months and years in the date display or on small dials.

Calibre: The measurement, in millimetres, which defines the dimensions of a watch movement.

Charge indicator: Mechanism indicating the life of a battery.

Complication: Any function not directly related to the simple telling of time. Also used to designate a watch which features one or many of these extra functions.

Complicated: Used to refer to a watch featuring one or many complications.

Display: The mechanism which indicates the time on a digital liquid crystal watch.

Escapement: The part of the mechanism which regulates force with relation to the balance, keeping it in oscillation via energy obtained from the mainspring. Different types of escapement include: verge escapement (in clocks), recoil escapement and the deadbeat escapement.

Electronic: A watch in which mechanical contact is replaced by a transistor.

Equation of time: The difference between real solar time and mean solar time, resulting from the Earth's erratic orbit. In the course of a year, the equation of time varies by about 16 minutes. Watches featuring an equation of time function are equipped with a mechanism to measure this difference.

Fly-back hand: A supplementary, independent second hand. Featured on chronographs and used for the simultaneous timing of two intervals in a single event (in sports, for example).

Frequency: In quartz watches, the frequency defines the movement's number of oscillations per second.

Function: Any operation linked to the measurement of time (chronography, date indication, etc.)

Grande Complication: In watchmaking, this term means that the master horologist has succeeded in combining a large number of complicated functions within a single watch. When a watch features several complications, it is a 'montre à grande complication', or a highly complicated watch.

Index: A mark used to indicate the hours on a dial.

Jewels: Very hard, industrial gems used within the movement to prevent wear and tear. The higher the number of jewels, the higher quality the watch.

Line: The most frequently used unit of measure for a calibre, corresponding to 2.555 millimetres (0.099 inches)

Lunar phase: The indication, usually in a display window, of successive aspects of the moon throughout its monthly cycle.

Manufacture: In the context of watchmaking, this term refers to companies that make the wheelworks which comprise the movement and case, and also assemble the watch.

Minute repeater: The complication to end all complications for master watchmakers. It is composed of a system which strikes a chime, via a push-piece or cursor. The most famous minute repetitions are those created by Audemars Piguet and Patek Philippe.

Perpetual calendar: An automatic calendar which takes into account the length of the months as well as leap years.

Perpetual day/date: The indication of the date with automatic regulation of the length of the months and leap years. Also used to designate a watch with a perpetual calendar.

Rotating bezel: A graduated, movable ring located on the upper part of the case, surrounding the dial.

Scale: Graduated marks along the dial, bezel or the exterior of the watch case which serve to measure speed, distance, etc.

Tantalum: Highly resistant blue-tinted metal which only melts at extreme temperatures.

Titanium: An extremely resilient corrosion-resistant white metal that is highly prized and more expensive than platinum.

Vibration: The oscillating movement of a piece from one extremity to the other. Two vibrations make up an oscillation. Usually, the balance of a watch produces 5 vibrations per second, which corresponds to 18,000 per hour, but this number can be higher.

Acknowledgements

We would like to thank the following people for their valuable assistance:

Monsieur Bernard Ravier of Audemars Piguet, Madame Marie-Laure Rozan of Baume & Mercier, Madame Nathalie Luneau of Breguet, Madame Caroline Pigeon and Madame Laurence Phitoussi of Breitling, Madame Anne Aufort, Madame Patricia Schiffbauer and Madame Sylvie Sarrazin of Cartier, Madame Jocelyne Ruault for Hamilton, Longines and Omega, Madame Catherine du Jeu of IWC, Madame Gisela Sagromski of A. Lange & Sohne, Madame Christine Pasquier of Jaeger LeCoultre, Monsieur Marco Richon of Omega, Madame Marie-Christine Blazin of Patek Philippe, Monsieur Didier Dauchy and Madame Stephanie Fleury of TAG Heuer, Monsieur Liebengut and Madame Ruffion of Zenith.

Thanks also to Madame Geneviève Aullen, of the French Watch and Clock Information Centre,
for her invaluable help in the translation of this work.

The photographs in this book were produced thanks to Monsieur Jean Lassaussois,
owner of three Les Montres boutiques in Paris, who kindly loaned us his precious timepieces.

Photographic credits

All photographs featured in this book are the work of Yvan Duton, with the exception of p. 24, courtesy Audemars Piguet press office; pp. 80 and 81, courtesy A. Lange & Söhne press office, pp. 104 and 105, courtesy Patek Philippe press office.

Produced by Copyright
Layout: Gabrielle Benhini
Editorial Collaboration: Hervé Borne
Coordination: Gracieuse Dardenne

Translation: Tina Isaac
English edition: Cathy Muscat